Holiday Bizarre

Holiday Bizarre

The Southern Indiana Writers' Group

Holiday Bizarre
Volume 17 of the Indian Creek Anthology Series

Published by Southern Indiana Writers, 2200 Reno Ave., New Albany, IN, 47150
Book designed by T. Lee Harris

ISSN 1085-357X
ISBN 978-0-9882664-0-7

Cover Art and design by T. Lee Harris

This book is dedicated to Genarose Turner, without whom there would be no Indian Creek Anthology Series.

Holiday Bizarre

Contents

Foreword .... Southern Indiana Writers

1 The Maltese Groundhog .... T. Lee Harris

13 Illustration ....T. Lee Harris

21 Beloved .... Dirk Griffin

22 Holiday .... Marian Allen

23 Illustration ....T. Lee Harris

24 Love Cats .... Dirk Griffin

25 Who Needs Roses? .... Bonnie Abraham

27 Illustration ....T. Lee Harris

28 Embryo .... Jeannine Baumgartle

29 Matin Pour Les Tombés .... Dirk Griffin

30 Francis, Tunnel Rat and Me .... Glenda Mills

38 Illustration ....T. Lee Harris

39 Fishing Holiday .... Jeannine Baumgartle

42 Photo ....Paula Harris

44 Lonnie, Me and the Battle of St. Crispin's Day .... Marian Allen

55 Illustration ....T. Lee Harris

59 Trick or Treat Night .... Jeannine Baumgartle

60 Feast of the Dead .... Ardis Moonlight

65 Illustration ....T. Lee Harris

67 Goldie .... Marian Allen

68 Illustration ....T. Lee Harris

69 Flor de Muerto .... Dirk Griffin

70 The Cautionary Tale of Silas Rockport .... Marian Allen

72 Illustration ....T. Lee Harris

74 Original Cover of Christmas Bizarre

75 The Christmas Pool .... Marian Allen

80 Illustration .... Joy Kirchgessner

84 The Christmas People .... Jeannine Baumgartle

86 Illustration .... Joy Kirchgessner

90 A Child-like Christmas .... Glenda Mills

91 The Feast of Stephen .... Ginny Fleming

96 When It's Christmastime Down South .... T. Lee Harris

97 A Tree out of Season .... Joy Kirchgessner

99 Visions of Sugarplums .... Ginny Fleming

109 Christmas in July .... Jeannine Baumgartle

110 Away in a Manger .... T. Lee Harris

119 The Touch of a Child .... Glenda Mills

128 Illustration .... Joy Kirchgessner

129 Tradition .... Marian Allen

131 Illustration .... Joy Kirchgessner and T. Lee Harris

132 Bethlehem .... Dirk Griffin

133 (Not So) Happy New Year .... Joanna Foreman

136 Photo ....Joanna Foreman

138 Recipe for Limoncello ....Joanna Foreman

139 Contributors

Foreword

Way back in the dim recesses of time — all the way back in 1996, the Southern Indiana Writers Group published *Christmas Bizarre*, volume 3 of the Indian Creek Anthology Series. It was a small book, only forty-seven pages long and it was the first time we'd used a computer to get a book ready for the printer. It was in chapbook form; what the printer referred to as a two-up saddle stitch.

Fast forward to 2012. (Yikes!) SIW has come a long way in the intervening years. Gained a few members; lost a few, cheered successes and mourned failures, but the group's Indian Creek Anthology Series is still chugging along with both new volumes and reprints of older editions.

When it came time to reprint *Christmas Bizarre*, we were a little dismayed at just how tiny it was. It was way too small to reprint as we had some of the others, so we decided to use it as the core of another anthology and surround it with new material taking in the entire calendar rather than just one holiday. In a way this book, *Holiday Bizarre*, can be seen as Southern Indiana Writers then and now. We hope the read is even more fun than the writing of it.

Enjoy!

Southern Indiana Writers' Group
April 1, 2012

The Maltese Groundhog

T. Lee Harris

The door opened, admitting three more patrons and buffeting Carroll McDermett with another blast of frigid January air. This was good news for Viv Tremane, the owner of the diner, but bad news for a guy just trying to stay warm. McDermett hunched his shoulders, laid his dog-eared book face down on the table and took a sip of the cooling coffee. Correction: *cold* coffee. He set the cup aside with a grimace and picked the book up again.

A shadow fell across the page. He looked up as Viv replaced his cold coffee with a fresh, hot cup. "If you didn't dawdle so, it wouldn't get cold." Her soft southern accent seemed at odds with the strident New York tones of her patrons' conversation. "It's warmer in the kitchen. Ah keep tellin' you that."

He laughed and shook his head. "No thanks. When I go into the kitchen I always seem to wind up washing dishes."

"That's because you're too cheap to buy your dinner any way else." She pointed to a folded newspaper on the seat beside him. "You gonna read that thing? Couple others want a look at it if you don't."

He handed it to her. "Why do I need to read it? I can tell you what it says. It's all that Hitler guy bullying someone else and all the politicos throwing presents at him hoping he'll stop. Won't work. Can't buy off a bully."

Wind gusted again, heralding another customer and the other patrons burst into a sudden chorus of wolf whistles and catcalls. Turning, Viv chuckled, "Talk about politicos. . . ."

Newly elected councilman Cameron McDermett, Carroll's elder brother, wearing full evening dress, closed the door against the wind, then stood momentarily self-conscious at the reception. Suddenly, he broke into a huge grin and swept the silk hat from his head in a deep bow. "Thank you, thank you, my constituents. I'll trust you to remember to cast your vote for McDermett in the next primary."

Laughing and joking with patrons all the way, he came back to Carroll's booth. "Heya, Viv. Business looks good."

"And you look like the cover of a Hollywood magazine. Where are you off to lookin' like Fred Astaire?"

"I've been invited to a reception at Gracie tonight. Big do for the upcoming World's Fair and you don't go into the presence of Mayor LaGuardia looking like a schlub."

"Don't want to go into the Presence half-frozen, neither. I'll get you a cup of hot coffee." She started away, remarking over her shoulder, "I'm afraid the silver service is out of the shop for cleaning. You'll have to make do with plain crockery like the rest of us plebeians."

Laughing, Cameron slid into the opposite bench from his brother, dropping his topper and silk scarf onto the table. "Now, why did I know I'd find you here?"

"Because I'm always here in the evening? Now, why did you want to find me in the first place? If you tell me Ma needs her toilet fixed again, I'll deck you, rented tux or no."

"Pop fixed it himself. Anyway, you can't hold me responsible for that, it was all Claire's doing. If you want to deck her, fine by me, but Ma will have something to say if you punch our sister."

Viv set a steaming cup on the table, then hurried off to tend another customer, leaving the brothers to talk in private.

Cameron cradled the cup appreciatively and said, "Actually, I came to tell you I may have a job for you."

Carroll looked skeptical. "Does it pay? That last fiasco at the Leiber jewelry promotion ended up costing *me*."

"That was all a misunderstanding. I got it back for you, didn't I?" At his brother's glare, he continued, "Look, this is cake. All you have to do is pick up a stuffed groundhog here in New York and deliver it to a friend of mine in Harrisburg, Pennsylvania."

"A stuffed *what*?"

"Groundhog. It's an animal — but it's dead. Otherwise it wouldn't be taxidermied."

Carroll rolled his eyes. "Okay. Let's try it this way: Why would someone pay me good money to take a dead groundhog to Pennsylvania? Deathbed wish?"

It was Cameron's turn to roll his eyes. "Remember Rudy Pearcy?"

"The guy you roomed with in law school?"

"That's the one."

"Wasn't he the one you got drunk with at Coney and—"

"*Yes.* That's him — anyway, he's working as an aide for the senior senator for Pennsylvania and his boss wants to present the critter to the mayor of Punxsutawney. Some sort of promotional thing. Groundhog Day, tourism, that sort of deal. Problem is, the senator wants a photo shoot with it before the presentation, but the taxidermist can't get it to them before the first of February. That's too late."

Carroll stared.

"If I can get this thing into Rudy's hands, it'll be big brownie points for him as well as me. Favor is a good thing in politics, little brother."

"They need me for this?"

"It's cash, Carroll."

At his brother's dubious grunt, Cameron withdrew his billfold, extracted a ten and slapped it onto the table. As it disappeared into Carroll's jacket pocket, he added, "Consider that a retainer. I'll get it back from Rudy later."

Noting the well-worn book between them, the elder McDermett prodded it. "You're not reading that thing again? You must have it committed to memory by now."

"Hey, this Hammett guy knows how it is. Being a private investigator isn't easy."

Cameron stirred sugar into his coffee and sipped thoughtfully. At length, he ventured, "Carroll. . . ."

"Ah. Here it comes."

Ignoring the comment, he continued, "Your name has been cleared, why don't you rejoin the police force?"

Carroll pursed his lips and regarded the scarred table top in silence.

"You were a great cop — decorated for bravery several times over. The force needs good men like you. I was talking to the Commissioner the other day—"

Carroll sat back and replied evenly, "Maybe you ought to point out to your pal the Commissioner that if he got rid of *all* the bad eggs, not just the ones who screw up publicly, maybe the good ones wouldn't stay away."

Cameron raised his hands in surrender against an old, unwinnable argument. "I know . . . it's just . . . well . . . you need a job."

"I *have* a job."

"One that *pays*."

"I'll have you know a client just gave me a ten dollar retainer."

For a moment, Cameron stared dumbfounded into his brother's impassive face, then burst out laughing. "All right. This round to you." He glanced at his watch and yelped, "Cripes. I'm gonna be late." Grabbing his hat and scarf, he stood and tossed a business card on the table. "There's the address of the shop. Mr. Schwarzkatze is expecting you around eight tomorrow morning."

Carroll picked up the card, then called after his fleeing sibling, "Expecting me?"

Cameron paused with his hand on the latch and called back, "Of course. I knew I could count on my baby brother. Drive safely!" With a jaunty wave, he plopped the silk topper on his head and was gone.

Carroll regarded the small card with a scowl. "Bastard."

# # #

The taxidermist's shop was in an older, slightly seedy part of town. McDermett guided the Packard to the curb, then got out and admired it for the umpteenth time. The sleek red Boattail Speedster was a 1930 model but, even at that age, would have been way beyond his means. It was one of the few things he still had to thank the New York Police Department for. He smiled, thinking back to what the car had looked like when he picked it up for a song, at auction. Cousin Dougal was a wizard at metalwork. You couldn't find the bullet holes now, even when you knew where to look.

He took a couple steps toward the door, then stopped cold. In the display window, squirrels played on a gnarled tree branch. An enchanting sight — until the realization struck home that everything in the window was dead. The bell over the door jangled cheerfully as he entered and a small, white-haired man behind the counter looked up from brushing the large black cat displayed on the counter. The man set the brush aside, and said, "Gut morning, mein Herr. What may I do to help you?"

When the cat stood up, stretched and yawned, McDermett took a startled step back. "Whoa! I thought the moggie was dead like these other critters."

The little man took off a pair of rimless spectacles and smiled. "Nein! Schatten is very much alive. He keeps me company in the long hours."

Rolling his shoulders uncomfortably under the glassy stares of the other denizens of the shop, McDermett said, "I can see why you wouldn't want to be alone too much."

The taxidermist smiled, "It is disconcerting to some, I think, but to me they are friends." The cat jumped down and rubbed against McDermett's trouser legs. "Ach. I hope you are not one who thinks the black cat is bad luck."

Carroll reached down and scratched the cat's head. "Not me. My parents are from the Scottish Highlands. A black cat is considered good luck there."

"Scotland?"

"Yeah, my whole family but me, really. I'm the first McDermett born in the United States."

"Of course, of course! You will be Councilman McDermett's brother. I talk to him yesterday. Your pardon that I did not realize this."

He waved the apology away. "No one ever pegs us as brothers. Has something to do with him being dark where I'm blond and him being tall where I'm . . . not so tall."

Grabbing Carroll's hand, the little man shook it enthusiastically. "I am Gustav Schwarzkatze — but you have probably already deduced this. Your brother tells me you are a detective. Most exciting!"

"Not usually. Mostly, it's very boring."

Covering his ears with both hands, Mr. Schwarzkatze said, "Nein! Do not disillusion an old man. I love the American detective writers Herr Hammett, Herr Van Dine . . . und the cinemas! James Cagney, Edward G. Robinson. Ach, but we waste time. You have a long journey ahead of you. The groundhog, he is still in the workroom. Come. Help me put him in his box and you can be on your way."

Carroll followed him through a curtained door into a cluttered workshop. "So you like S.S. Van Dine, huh? I dunno, I always thought Philo Vance needed a good sock in the nose. Sam Spade's more my kind of guy."

The groundhog stood in the center of a worktable, posed on its hind feet, front paws curled against its body with head slightly cocked. The wooden pedestal it was mounted on was a work of art in itself, solid cherry with beautifully worked sides. Across the room, Mr. Schwarzkatze rummaged around another bench, his running commentary slightly muffled. "I am terribly sorry to impose on you, Herr McDermett, but I am not as strong as I used to be and lifting him by myself is out of the question." He straightened, holding a large pasteboard box. "My assistant — my nephew Heinrich — has gone off with his rowdy friends again. He is not much help, but he is good at woodwork."

"He and his pals like to tear it up a bit?"

"That it would be so simple! These young people, they get together and badmouth America. I do not understand this. Heinrich was born in the US and doesn't know what hardship really is. His father and I, we come from Austria back in the twenties; it was hard here, but harder there. We struggle to make a life in this new country. There are many opportunities here that we would never have in the Old Country. Heinrich does not. . . ." He shook himself slightly and put his spectacles on, adding, "But that is not our business, ya? Our business is getting this fellow to his new home and since he is big, Heinrich has made a special box for him to travel in."

As Schwarzkatze plunked the pasteboard box onto the table, Schatten leapt effortlessly from the floor and disappeared into it. The taxidermist swore in German, then said, "It seems I do nothing but apologize to you, Herr McDermett. He has been doing this since my nephew finished constructing the box."

McDermett laughed. "No problem, Mr. Schwarzkatze. Cats are like that." As he lifted the cat out, he saw a white diamond-shaped patch on the animal's chest. Ruffling the white fur with his thumb, he remarked, "Oh. Cat Sidhe, are you?"

"Pardon? Caught she? It is a him."

"Oops, sorry. Cat Sidhe is an old Scottish legend about large black cats with white markings on their chests. They were believed to have been fairy folk or transformed witches."

The cat laid back battle-notched ears, squirmed out of his hands, groomed perfunctorily, then stomped away. Chuckling, the little man watched the exit. "I believe you are correct. Schatten has done remarkable things. He stopped a break in last week!"

"Break in? Who'd want to break into a taxidermy shop?"

"They perhaps thought there would be money, but I am a poor man and they found nothing. One of them, it seems, stepped on Schatten and he took exception. I live upstairs and the commotion woke me. I call the police."

"They catch the guys?"

"Nein. They were long gone when the police get here." He touched a spot on the groundhog's back. "I was much worried, though. In the confusion, the piece was damaged. It was a clean slit, so I was able to repair him. It can not be seen, ya?"

"Looks great to me, Mr. Schwarzkatze."

After some maneuvering, they finally got the bulky thing into the box. Carroll dusted his hands. "That's a snug fit. Good thing about it, he won't shift around much in the car."

"Ya. Heinrich builds good boxes, too. Please, could you get me the roll of string? It is on the counter in the front. I will get the lid and you will be ready to go."

A few minutes later, Carroll was carefully guiding his armful to the front door of the shop. Mr. Schwarzkatze opened the door, his final admonishment mixing with the bell's jangle. "Have care, Herr McDermett, he is heavy. My nephew has made a special strong box for him, but do not trust the bottom, ya?"

♯ ♯ ♯

The drive to Harrisburg looked to be long, but pleasant. In spite of the January cold outside, once the Packard warmed up, the interior was fairly comfortable. He loved driving the Speedster, Viv had packed a nice lunch, most of the roads were paved and he was getting paid for the lot. All in all, he couldn't complain.

Traffic became heavier as the day wore on. By early afternoon, he was looking for a spot to pull over to check his maps and break into the box lunch. Before long, he caught sight of a small park down the hill from the road. It was probably a pleasant picnic spot in summer, but in late January, it was pretty bleak, ringed by now-leafless trees and shrubs poking out of melting snow banks. Regardless, the turnoff was convenient and he was more concerned with taking a break than sightseeing.

The Packard rolled down the graveled drive and came to a smooth halt at the bottom. Even leafless, the shrubs provided a decent privacy screen and he groped on the floor for the folded map and the lunch. His fingers met empty air. The box and maps had slid out of reach during the drive and the big box containing the groundhog wouldn't let him easily get to where they'd come to rest. There was nothing for it, he'd have to get out.

Muttering that a two seat roadster wasn't the best choice to transport a big anything, he stomped around the car. The passenger door had swung wide when he heard something large coming up behind him — fast. Breath whooshed out of him as he was grabbed, lifted off his feet and slammed hard against the trunk of the Speedster. He slid to the ground, only to be lifted again by a vicious kick to the ribs, then rolled away from the next blow. The passing of his attacker's leather-soled shoe ruffled his hair. Landing on his back, he got a look at his opponent and almost wished he hadn't. The man would have been huge even without the heavy overcoat. From the parts of his face visible above the scarf he wore like a mask, he was no stranger to fighting and his glaring eyes were cold blue. The scarf twitched and McDermett had the uncomfortable feeling an unfriendly smile was spreading. All that became secondary, though, with the appearance of a very large, very ugly knife. The giant took a slow step forward as a voice rang out, "Bear!"

The cold blue eyes flicked toward the shout, and a part of McDermett snickered. This guy would have a monicker like that. He wondered idly if it was a name or a nickname.

The speaker continued his sliding progress down the drive, one hand holding a woolen scarf over his face and the other in his pocket. "Bear! That's enough."

No need to speculate what the pocket held, because as the other, smaller man skidded to a breathless halt, he produced a nickel-plated automatic from it and aimed it down at Carroll.

McDermett's eyes slid toward the Packard where his .35 service pistol was. In the glove box. With a dead groundhog on top of it.

"Get up. Slow," the gunman ordered.

With a groan, McDermett complied. His abused ribs assured the rise would be nothing but slow.

The pistol followed his progress and the man remarked conversationally, "You're a hard guy to keep up with, McDermett. Lucky for us that roadster of yours is easy to spot."

"Yeah. Real lucky, Mr. . . . ?"

"That's none of your business. Just stay out of the way and you won't get hurt any worse."

"I'm all for that."

"Glad you see things our way. I heard you were a smart guy." The dark eyes never moved from McDermett's face as he snapped, "Bear, you know what we're here for. Since you have your toothpick out, why don't you get it?"

For a moment, the big man wavered, pinning McDermett with a hate-filled glare, daring him to flinch. When that didn't happen, he turned to the open car and slit the string securing the lid with more force than absolutely necessary. The knife disappeared under his coat and he reached in. Suddenly, the lid exploded backward. With an unearthly wail, the groundhog seemed to rise from the box and wrap itself around the big man's head.

The giant's shrieks and the creature's screams bounced off the skeletal trees and McDermett stood momentarily frozen open-mouthed. Shaking himself free of the shock, he swung on the gunman. His fist connected solidly with the small man's scarf-covered nose. Bright red soaked yellow wool as the man staggered back. In an instant, McDermett had the pistol and wheeled just in time to see Bear pry the creature loose and fling it into the shrubs, his face a mass of blood. Snarling, he lunged for the weapon in Carroll's hand.

The automatic spat fire and Bear clutched his side with a renewed roar.

"There's more where that came from, fellas."

The smaller man, still sprawled on the ground, swung his legs around, catching McDermett at ankle level, pitching him sideways. He lost his grip on the automatic as he hit the ground. The other man pounced on it, then sprang up shouting something unintelligible.

The two men pelted up the hill leaving red trails in their wake. McDermett lay in the slush for a moment weighing whether to get up or just lie there. In the end, he pulled himself painfully to his feet and leaned against the still-warm Packard as the sound of another car gunning into traffic reached him. He was still cataloging his injuries when something leapt onto the hood next to him and butted his shoulder. Startled, he bounced away and looked back to see a large black cat sitting on the hood of the car. The cat shook itself and started grooming its wet fur. As it turned, McDermett caught the flash of a white diamond-shaped blaze.

"Schatten? But how. . . ?" Glancing toward the now-open box with the groundhog motionless inside, he slapped his forehead. "Of course! *You* were in the box. So much was happening I didn't stop to think. . . ."

He sagged back against the Speedster. "Well, pal, looks like you foiled another robbery attempt — or something. But why in hell would anyone want to steal a dead groundhog?" The cat stared, then hopped down, jumped into the car and sat as if waiting.

McDermett started to shoo the animal out, then stopped. This wasn't just some stray cat, this was Mr. Schwarzkatze's pet. The old guy was probably frantic looking for him. No way could he dump Schatten in the middle of nowhere. It would kill the little guy to lose his friend like that. Okay. Next service station, he'd call and let him know where Schatten was — right after he called Cameron and read him the riot act for getting him involved in yet another harebrained fiasco.

♯ ♯ ♯

It took a while to reach a place big enough to have a pay phone he could use. Fortunately, the booth was located where he could keep an eye on the idling Packard while he waited to be put through to his brother's law offices in New York. He could just make out Schatten perched on the big box. More to the point, he could see the cat's gleaming eyes and catch the flash of the white diamond.

At length, he heard his brother's voice on the line, "Carroll! Where are you?"

Carroll snarled, "How should I know? Somewhere in Pennsylvania. Why do I let you talk me into these things? I keep telling myself, 'say no, keep saying no' but—"

"Carroll, what the hell are you talking about? If I accepted reverse long distance charges just so you could grouse at me, I'll take it out of your hide!"

"Too late, somebody already did that. Who in hell wants a dead groundhog, I don't know, but you didn't tell me someone would be willing to beat the beejebus out of me and threaten to carve me up or shoot me for it."

"Someone followed you and beat you up? This worries me."

"Worries YOU? Not half as much—"

"No, whoa! Carroll, listen to me."

The answer was more a growl than an okay, but Cameron hurried on. "Listen, I was just hearing on the radio that the guy you picked the critter up from this morning, Mr. Schwarzkatze, was found dead in his shop. Shot. Looked like a robbery, but now I'm not so sure."

Reality slowed for a moment. The cat pawed at the car window. "Damn."

"Maybe you better turn back. The police might want to talk to you since you're probably the last person who spoke with him."

"I dunno. As far as I've come, it'll be closer for me to go on to Harrisburg. On top of it all, I have the guy's cat."

"You have what?"

"Mr. Schwarzkatze's shop cat. It must have jumped in the box when we were packing the thing. Jumped out when the goons attacked. . . ." His words trailed off as three men strolled up to

the Packard. He was used to that. There weren't many of the Boattail Speedsters around and it frequently attracted attention. Still, there was something strange in the way these three approached.

Cameron was saying, "That's screwy, Carroll."

"Tell me about it." The men were looking in the windows of the car and he could see Schatten flashing around inside. "Look, I gotta go. Something's come up."

Cameron protested, but he didn't hear the words. The buzzing cut off abruptly as the receiver clicked home into the cradle. He hurried outside. As he approached the trio, he heard one of them insisting, "I tell ya, Armstrong, it's that same damned cat!"

A man built along the same lines as a brick outhouse waved dismissively. "Ah, you're full of it. You got cats on the brain, Bowen."

McDermett arced around so he was closer to the driver's side and the bulk of the Packard was between himself and the men. "Good afternoon, fellas."

They looked up as one, then Armstrong asked, "This your car?"

The cat hissed, slunk to the side of the big box and meowed plaintively at McDermett, then disappeared to the floorboards. "It is. Looks like you fellas are upsetting the cat."

The man who'd been addressed as Bowen straightened up from glaring in the window. A set of deep scratches was healing along his left cheek and neck. "That your cat?"

"Belongs to a friend of mine. Maybe I should say 'belonged' seeing how my friend is dead. He doesn't seem to like you much."

The other two edged around the car in opposite directions. He let his hands drop casually to his sides, loose, ready to move. After the dust up at the roadside stop, he wasn't about to get caught flat-footed again.

The guy to his right snarled, "I think you better come with us."

"I think I'd rather not."

The man to his left slipped slightly behind him. A blur of motion at the edge of his vision triggered an instinctive dodge and he used his momentum to carry him into the big guy to his right, knocking him sprawling. The other man raised his sap again, but dropped it fast when McDermett's kick came up for a solid impact. He sank to his knees and Carroll scooped the sap from the icy gravel, whirled and laid it against Armstrong's head. Bowen launched himself, but Carroll ducked and brought the sap down on the base of the man's neck. No one was out, but they were hurting. Time to put distance between him and them.

He jumped into the car and gunned the engine, spraying the scrambling men with slush and gravel. As they bumped back onto the road, Schatten crept onto the seat and huddled against him. McDermett glanced down, then back at the road. "This is getting interesting, cat. Too bad you can't talk."

⌗ ⌗ ⌗

It was dark and far too late to stop by the senator's office when he hit Harrisburg. He wasn't sure that was such a good idea, anyway. He wished he'd seen the cars the goons came in, but he hadn't. The rearview mirror kept pulling his eyes, anyway.

He drove aimlessly through the city until he was sure no one was following, then cut through to the opposite side and into the outlying areas, where he found a cheap motor lodge with a scattering of bungalows. He rented one away from the road, pulled the Packard behind it and got out to stretch. The cold air hit him like a slap in the face. That was okay. He couldn't afford to be fuzzy-headed. He thought he'd lost them all, but still. . . .

Schatten leapt lightly from the car onto the refreezing ground and padded straight for the tree line. McDermett watched for a moment then, took his bag and the still untouched lunch and, with a backward glance at the Packard, turned for the cabin. His .35 caliber service pistol was still in the car blocked by the oversized box. It would come in with the groundhog. He'd been caught unarmed two times, he wasn't looking to make it three. The cat shot through as he opened door and hopped onto the bed. Carroll started to protest, but relented. It was too damned cold out for a poor moggie. He snapped the lights on, saying, "All right. I won't throw you out, but you better keep your nose clean or we'll both be out in the street."

The cat yawned and busied himself cleaning snow from between his toes.

Once the groundhog was inside and the Speedster locked up, McDermett sank onto the bed and shared the food with Schatten. It was cold, but welcome after the long day. He hadn't realized just how hungry he was until he took the first bite of chicken.

The cat was licking the plate clean when McDermett finally sat back sipping at the tepid coffee from the thermos, staring at the box with the groundhog. "I'm thinking we just might want to look Mr. Hog over, now that we have a little privacy. Maybe I can see what the interest is in it."

He set the cup on the bedside table and stood, just as the cat laid his ears back and growled at the door. Carroll froze and reached for the .35. The door exploded inward and slammed against the wall as the unmistakable form of the man called Bear hurtled into the room. He plowed into McDermett, crashing him to the floor. Weapon drawn, the small man followed swiftly. He'd only gone a few steps before a black streak launched from under the bed and attached itself to his face, ripping the scarf away. McDermett barely registered it, because Bear had his hands around his throat, squeezing and banging his head against the floorboards.

Suddenly as it all began, Bear was pulled away. Sitting up shakily, Carroll saw Armstrong from the roadside diner slamming Bear face down onto the floor and cuffing his hands behind him. Taking a deep breath, McDermett came up swinging only to be stopped by a badge in his face. "Simmer down, McDermett. We're the good guys. Agent MacLane, FBI."

Snatching the shield from MacLane, he glared at it. "FBI, is it? Would have been nice if you'd told me that down the road instead of trying to bash my skull in."

The agent took the identification and tucked it back into his jacket pocket. "Yeah, well, how did we know you weren't with these jokers? Wasn't until we ran your plates, we found out you were a good egg."

McDermett's response was cut off as Bowen yanked the gunman off the floor. "Well, well! Heinrich Schwarzkatze. We been wanting to talk to you. Should have known we'd find you when we found Stefan Baer."

MacLane walked over to the box. "So this is what all the fuss is about. What the hell is it, anyway?"

"It's a stuffed groundhog some senator wants for a publicity thing," McDermett said.

MacLane lifted the lid and peered in. "Yep. It's a dead critter all right. That has to be the dumbest thing I ever heard."

Carroll shrugged. "It's politics."

"Yeah. Like I was sayin'. . . . Bowen, shut that door if you can, no reason for us all to freeze to death."

McDermett winced as Bowen forced the door closed. It worked, but just. Baer's entrance had done bad things to the hinges and frame. Somebody was gonna pay through the nose for that. It was definitely cold out, but he doubted the occupants of the small room could have frozen even if there was a blizzard raging. The tiny one-room bungalow wasn't designed to hold six men and a cat — he was damned glad he wasn't claustrophobic. He pulled a straight-backed chair around and straddled it, chuckling, "And here, I thought I lost everyone but good."

MacLane looked up. "Actually, you did. You lost us back at the diner, but while we were standing in the parking lot cursing you, who should wander in but Stefan Baer? He looked a little worse for it, too. Kinda like you, Bowen."

Bowen glared and spat, "Damn cat. Black as the ace of spades. Who coulda seen him, I ask ya?"

Realization dawned. "So you guys were old man Schwarzkatze's burglars! What were you doing poking around a taxidermist's workroom, anyway?"

MacLane indicated the groundhog. "I think we were looking for this. The New York office got a tip that Nazi sympathizers were using the shop for a drop point. We thought we'd have ourselves a little look-see. Didn't get very far. Bowen stepped on the cat and brought the house down on us."

McDermett shook his head. "You can't convince me that Gustav Schwarzkatze would throw in with that bunch of goose-stepping bullies. He loved this country too much for that."

"Not Gustav. Heinrich." MacLane glared at the sullen gunman and continued, "You're right about Gustav, too. He was all right. We figure Heinrich, here, offed him when he found out what Heinrich and his little friends were really up to. Was that it, Heinie? Might as well tell us, we'll get it out of you sooner or later."

Heinrich Schwarzkatze snarled, "Stuff yourself, G-Man."

"Awwwww. Ain't he tough?" MacLane grinned. "Anyway, Armstrong was calling in your tags when this beauty strolled in. We couldn't get a good look at his pal in the car, but from Bear's look, we figured he'd had a good tangle. We just hitched onto their tail and followed them around."

Armstrong laughed. "They hit every motel and motor lodge around here looking for that snazzy car of yours. Getting pretty cranky toward the end, too."

Stefan Baer cut loose with a string of swearing. Armstrong shouted him down. "Hey, watch your mouth, you mug. What would your mother say?"

MacLane continued calmly, "So when they found you, we just followed them to the door. The rest is history."

McDermett worked his neck. "Painful history. Now what?"

"Hey, Armstrong. Get over here and make yourself useful. Let's get our furry pal out."

The groundhog didn't come out of the box any easier than he went in, but after a brief struggle, it stood on the table, triumphantly boxless, and the carton was tossed onto the floor. McDermett joined the FBI men around the table as they treated the stuffed animal to a through examination until MacLane looked up and asked, "What's that cat doing?"

Schatten had made a run at the box and dived in. He then proceeded to scratch at the sides and bottom punctuating the shredding with a series of mush-mouthed meows.

Armstrong waved dismissively. "Ah, it's nothing, my wife's cat does the same thing."

Bowen announced, "You're nuts. That cat's gonna crap all over the place. Get it outta here."

Suddenly, everyone was looking at McDermett. "Hey, what gives?"

Armstrong said, "Well, it's sort of your cat, ain't it?"

McDermett sighed and glanced toward the discarded carton. All that was visible of Schatten was the tip of his tail that quivered with his enthusiastic digging. Just beyond, Schwarzkatze and Baer sat back to back watching the agents prodding the groundhog; Heinrich wore a surprisingly smug smile. The shredding ceased abruptly and the cat poked his head over the edge, riveting Carroll with intense green eyes; bits of pasteboard clung to his whiskers. Schwarzkatze's and McDermett's eyes met over the animal's head and the small man's pinched face suddenly lost its smugness.

"So it's like that, is it?" Two steps and he had hold of the box sides. He jerked it off the floor in one quick motion. With a loud pop, the bottom fell out, raining cat, shreds of tape and pasteboard and long tendrils of film to the floor.

Bowen pointed. "Hey lookit! McDermett's got it!"

The agents crowded around, whooping happily and pounding Carroll on the back. McDermett watched Schatten as he strolled across the room, hopped onto the table next to the groundhog and turned his gaze on Schwarzkatze. It had to be imagination, but the cat looked – victorious.

MacLane brought his attention back by jabbing him in the shoulder, saying: "If I say let's go back to HQ now, you gonna slug me again, McDermett?"

"Not as long as there's hot coffee and someone agrees to pay for the door."

MacLane laughed. "That can probably be arranged. Might be able to find a dram or two of Scotch, if we try."

McDermett treated Heinrich to a brilliant smile, and ruffled Schatten's black fur. "Sounds good. And maybe we can even find a bit of milk for the moggie."

The Maltese Groundhog originally appeared at Mysterical-E.

Beloved
Dirk Griffin

Between the silences of breaths and dreams
I bless these moments you bestow on me.
For we are golden under stars or sun,
or even beneath clouds where thunder rolls.

And time has only strengthened our heart-bonds
by trials that test these truths and mark our way.
In darkness I will ever turn to you,
to strike the fire that ever lights our way.

Though many fear to trust themselves to this,
this song that joins our hearts, our minds, our souls;
it is the only thing that I have found
which makes a life feel worthy to be lived.

There are so many words that I could say,
but none will match the love you've brought my way.

Holiday

Marian Allen

It had snowed the day before. Most of the park was invisible; dangerously out of sight. Thick clouds seemed to cup the space like a huge hand over a novelty sticker; halogen lights tricked out to resemble gas lamps gleamed feebly, like spots of luminescent paint. Uneven ground was muffled in drifts. From where the young man waited, in the center of the park, only a few irregular yards were clearly visible; the rest was hidden by darkness, by convolutions of the ground, by growth, by shadow, by dry-stone walls, by warning signs and litter barrels.

The snow itself was churned and dirtied out of recognition as "snow." No sparkle in the lamplight. No lack of spots to put a foot and leave no tell-tale track.

"The trailing hand of God leaves a wake of perfection," said the boy, and ducked his head and sniggered.

The young man was of no certain age; he might have been overgrown for minor years or stunted in full growth. His eyes brimmed with delight and sparked with impersonal malice. He had with him a bow which he alone could pull, and a quiver of red-fletched arrows. The silver arrowheads were barbed, and dull with their dried coating.

There were no targets in the park that midnight; a damp cold — not bitter, but sour — had turned even the romance of random cruelty in upon itself.

The boy settled in, unwrapping and eating the food he'd brought from home, and waited.

As the sun rose, so did the archer. He stretched, loosened his muscles, and tightened his bowstring. He nocked an arrow. He crouched. He waited.

A man and a woman approached, talking with the ease of

long- standing friendship. They talked about their jobs, their apartments in the same building, one's cats, one's lack of cats. The archer stuck a second shaft loosely into the snow before him and drew his bow. By the time the man had read the arrow's message in the woman's eyes, another was in his heart.

By the time the next targets came, the first were gone.

The day passed with pleasant swiftness for the boy. Quarry came thick sometimes; sometimes someone saw something, took some notice, but no one interfered. There were those who smiled and nodded.

Night came, as did one old man who grumbled, as he took the longest path, of a wife he'd never cared for, and cursed her clear affection.

"Someone's in for a lovely surprise," said the boy, while his arrow whispered, "Yesss."

The archer shouldered his weapon. The liquid cold washed through the empty park. The boy's eyes were vacant of time as his heart crooned over the day's count.

The courthouse clock struck twelve; the young man departed.

February 14th was over for another year. Olympus welcomed its vacationing boy, Eros, Cupid, home.

Holiday has also appeared at MarianAllen.com, in Literally (The Writers' Center of Indianapolis' newsletter), and in Serendipity Systems' Serendipity Sampler.

Love Cats

Dirk Griffin

the air is blue with smoke
slow Jazz hums low and sweet
an urgent shallow beat
sharing a gauzy toke

love cats we stalk the night
sultry brown eyes hunting
no need to be fronting
it's passion we ignite

notes fade, dissolve away
as sun licks nighttime's edge
don't need to make no pledge
walking from your stairway

from dusk to dawn delight
the old established rite
our days will have no sun
'cause love cats love as one

Who Needs Roses?
Bonnie Abraham

I have never liked grocery shopping, so I wasn't in a very good mood to begin with. Seeing all the red hearts and roses for Valentine's Day — even in the grocery store, for pity sakes — hadn't improved my attitude. So when I saw Joe Alender in the checkout line in front of me, paying for a big box of candy and a bunch of roses, maybe you can understand when I say it made me feel sorry for myself. See, Joe Alender once asked me to marry him.

It was forty years ago, when we were still in high school. We had a whirlwind romance that lasted about three weeks. When I told him I wasn't ready to get married, he dropped me and started dating Mary Rodgers. My Billy asked me out to the next dance and that was that.

Billy and I have been married thirty-eight years. Now don't get me wrong, Billy is a good man and I love him — but a romantic he is not. He has never given me flowers or a box of candy, or even a card for Valentine's Day. We've never gone out for a fancy dinner by candlelight. And when I tried to have one at home, Billy got up and turned on the lights. "I like to see my food," was all he said, so I never tried it again. I love Billy, but a girl sometimes craves just a *little* romance.

"I'm not asking for a trip to Hawaii — just a card, maybe," I grumbled, as I got in my car and drove home. Billy, I knew, wouldn't even *remember* it was Valentine's Day. I put the groceries away and started supper, still feeling sorry for myself.

I was peeling carrots for the roast when the phone rang. "Milly, you'll never guess—" It was my best friend Clara. If you ever want to know what's going on in town, just find Clara and she'll fill you in on everything. I have never figured out how she finds out all this gossip, but she's seldom wrong.

"Hi, Clara," I said, breaking into her latest breathless tidbit.

"Oh. Hi, Milly. You'll just never—"

"Probably not, so tell me."

"Well, I saw Martha in the dress shop, (she was trying on the most awful green dress) and she said Carol Ann told her (they're speaking to each other again) she heard that Joe and his wife are splitting up. What is that? Wife number three?"

"Four," I said.

"Anyway, seems she found him kissing his *secretary*. Just like *last* time. You'd think the man would *learn*!"

"Not Joe," I said. "I wonder who the flowers were for."

"What?"

"Oh, nothing." We talked a few minutes more then, having sufficiently scalded Joe Alender with our tongues, we said our good-byes and I went back to work on the carrots.

I thought of Joe's four wives. Each of them gave him sons. Always the romantic, he showered them with flowers and candy and fancy dinners during their brief times together. And then left each of them for the next one. He always paid the alimony and child support payments on time, but he never paid any attention to his boys or asked if they needed anything.

The phone rang again. It was Billy.

"I'm gonna be a little late for dinner. I need to run by Sarah's place and see what's wrong with her water heater. She said Matt tried to fix it and now there's water everywhere. She's pretty upset. Something about it spoilin' some special evening."

See, I told you he wouldn't remember what day it was. "Dinner's no problem," I said. "I'm fixing a roast, so it will hold. Give Sarah a hug for me and tell her—" I stopped as an idea hit me. It *was* Valentine's Day, and I had that roast cooking. "Tell them to come over here for supper. I'll get out the good dishes."

I hung up the phone and smiled. I'd set the table in the dining room for them and at least *they* could eat by candlelight. As I prepared the dining room, I recalled the tiredness in Billy's voice. He had gone in to work early to get some extra overtime so we could afford to fix the roof. I knew his back was hurting. It always does — too much heavy lifting. Overtime almost cripples him.

"Whatever were you thinking, Milly Zucher," I said to myself. "Who needs roses and chocolates when you have a hero like Billy for a husband?"

Embryo

Jeannine Baumgartle

I am the center of Easter
    Life warm readiness
The nucleus that needs protecting

Wars have been fought
    Innocents punished
That my dream
    Be not disturbed

I call myself awake
    Golden rise in shallow water
Hardened into thought

Already cramped
    I rest and fling
Rest and fling
    Fall out

I know you now
    Trust my fragile footing
In your palm

You let me go
    I'm sorry
Wanting to understand
    The scars

Matin Pour Les Tombés

Dirk Griffin

My love of sin
dark, moonless
fills my nights

Hear me O, Lord
Incline to me

even as my heart
sighs I bring myrrh
kiss your feet wet;
dry them clean with
my unworthy hair

Hear me O, Lord,
Incline to me

You have gathered
the waters of the earth
bowed the heavens
bring now light to
my darkness

I know the fear
that gripped
Eve's heart
hearing your
footsteps echoing
in her sin

Hear me O, Lord
incline to me

Know the shadows
in my soul
in the twilight
of paradise
bearing myrrh
to your tomb
knowing your judgments
will find the
depths of my sins

Yet still I seek you
in love
still I seek you
in purity
I would be your handmaiden

Hear me O, Lord
Incline to me
only your mercy
can be greater than
my fall

Francis, Tunnel Rat and Me

Glenda Mills

I'd known Marty for a little over a year. He was a regular guest at the soup kitchen where I volunteer on Friday nights. He stood about five feet tall, but the weight of survival crushing down on his shoulders made him seem even shorter. He always wore blue jeans and a black T-shirt with POW/MIA in white letters across the top. There was a picture of a soldier underneath the letters and under that the words, "Never forgotten." He had a beard and long salt-and-pepper hair that he usually wore pulled back from his face. He didn't say much when he came through the line. Most everyone at the kitchen knew him as Tunnel Rat, a nickname he'd earned while serving in Vietnam.

The first night Marty showed up at the soup kitchen with Francis by his side, the director told him that Francis could not stay. Don't get me wrong. We never turn away a hungry person, but Francis wasn't human. He was a dog, and not just any dog. He was a beautiful white pit bull, probably two or three years old. He had one brown eye and one blue eye and both of them looked up at me with the same longing as the children I saw from week to week. I lived next door to the church, so I told Marty I had an idea. We went over to my house. I was searching for a way to secure Francis when I heard Marty say, "Stay." I looked over and Francis was curled up on my front porch like he belonged there.

"Should we tie him up or something?" I asked.

"Nope. He'll stay there until I come back. He does just what I tell him. He and I have a special bond."

With that, Marty walked back over to the dining hall. I took one look down at the white lump lying in front of my door. "You'd best be here when Marty gets back," I warned, pointing my finger at the dog and shaking it. "Don't you cause no trouble, now." Francis lifted his head and sighed heavily, then settled back down for a nap.

After the food was served, the dishes washed, the floors swept and mopped, and the trash and lights put out, I headed back across the alley. I was thinking more about the roast I had in the crock-pot and the Jan Karon novel I couldn't wait to get back to than the presence of a pit bull on my porch. But sure enough, there he was. And he wasn't alone. Marty was sitting on my swing, swaying gently in the cool breeze of the September evening. He stopped when he saw me coming and stood up.

"I hope you don't mind me sticking around for a while. I really just wanted to thank you for being so nice to Francis. He's a good dog, but people don't seem to like him much."

I motioned for Marty to sit back down. I joined him on the porch, seating myself in my rocking chair on the other side. Francis came over and put his front paws in my lap. When he lifted himself up, his face was right even with mine. Next thing I knew, I had my first ever pit bull kiss. It was wet and sloppy, not much different from the first time Harley had kissed me back in high school.

"Francis, no. That's not polite. Get over here right now." Marty's voice was firm, but I could see a smile on his face. Francis paused and looked at me as if to say, "Sorry, but I gotta go," then he dropped down from my lap, walked over to the swing and put his head on Marty's knee. Marty petted him a few times, and then turned his attention back to me.

"You sure are a nice person. I knew that even before tonight. Francis can sense it, too. He don't kiss just anybody."

"I'm flattered, really. You know the director wasn't trying to be unkind. He just can't have animals in the dining hall or kitchen. If the health department got wind of it, we'd be in a heap of trouble. They might even shut us down. I'm just glad I live so close and Francis minds so well."

"Yeah, he's a good boy. I wish everybody else would give him the same chance you did."

"I don't see why they wouldn't. Has he done something wrong?"

"No, but he's a pit bull so he don't have to do anything. Just being what he is makes people treat him bad."

"How did you end up with him, anyway? I haven't seen him with you before."

Francis left Marty, made three circles in front of my screen door and lay down, his head resting on his paws. My welcome mat disappeared beneath him.

"He found me about a week ago. I was camped out under the interstate up by the golf course on Cherry. I had done some yard work for a lady that day, so I went to the store to get some food. When I came back, he was sitting on my sleeping bag. I fed him some bologna and gave him some water. Then I went to bed. Figured he'd make up his own mind whether to stay or not. I woke up the next morning, and there he was, curled up beside me. He ain't left my side since."

"Seems to me you've got a friend."

"Seems like it. You know, I don't have anybody else." Marty paused for a moment, looked down at Francis, and suddenly he was a thousand miles away from my porch, somewhere only he could see. "Doing what I did in 'Nam changed me. I can't stand confined spaces. The nightmares come almost every night. If a car backfires, I fall to the ground because I think it's a mortar round exploding. A man never really comes home. The war follows you, haunts you. Most people see me the same way they see Francis there — mean, scary, unstable. Maybe that's why he and I are so close. We both know what it's like to be hated just because people don't understand."

I knew Marty was right. Even at the soup kitchen, the others shied away from him. His behavior could be erratic, especially when he would mumble to himself for long periods of time or carry on conversations with people who he apparently could see but no one else could.

"You know, my Harley never really came home, either."

For the first time since his mind had wandered away, he looked at me and I knew he was back on my front porch. "Who's Harley?"

Now it was my turn to slip away, not to another place, mind you, but to another time, a time when Harley had just come home from the second War to End All Wars. "Harley was my husband. He died on Memorial Day, five years ago this coming May. I remember him waking up at night screaming, reliving some hell on earth. I remember him warning me not to sneak up on him unannounced, and I remember the time I forgot his warning and he nearly stabbed me with a screwdriver. I remember how much he hated the sound of fireworks and how when he'd drink, he'd cry, not only for his buddies who didn't come home, but for his enemies and their families as well." For a minute or so, both of us stopped and rested inside our own heads.

"So," I said, figuring it was a good time to change the subject, "who in the world could have it in for such a sweetheart as Francis?"

"I share space under the overpass with one of the other guys who eats here on Fridays. He's a big man, always wears a jacket, no matter what the weather is. He has dark hair."

I nodded my head. "I don't know why, but he makes me nervous. I try not to judge any of the folks who show up here, but he's different somehow. It's not that I think badly of him, but I just feel uneasy when he comes through the line."

"You know why he wears that jacket all the time, don't you? He's packing."

It took me a few seconds to connect the slang with a meaning. "You mean he carries a gun on him when he comes to eat here?"

"He carries a gun all the time. The first morning he woke up and saw Francis, he shot at him. I asked him what he thought he was doing, shooting at my dog, and he said he wasn't having no pit bull hanging around. Said all pits were mean. I told him the only one being mean was him, and he'd best leave Francis alone. Things have been tense between us since. I ain't scared for myself. Francis wouldn't let anything happen to me, but I sure do worry about him. That's why I named him Francis. I'm counting on St. Francis to help me keep him safe until I can find a different place for us to stay."

"Well, I can tell you this much. Francis has a place to go on Friday nights for sure. You can bring him here anytime, and you are welcome to visit as well."

Marty stood up. "Thank you, ma'am."

"It's Karen."

Marty nodded. "Thank you, Karen. Francis, come on, boy. We got to go. We'll come back next week and see our friend again."

Francis stretched, yawned, and came over to me. I hugged his neck and got another kiss, this time on the top of my hand. Then Marty and Francis turned and left, side by side, down the sidewalk toward the overpass.

For weeks after that, Marty, Francis and I met on my front porch every Friday night after dinner. Marty got Francis a leash, hoping it would ease the tension between him and his neighbor. I told him it was a good idea, because by law Francis was supposed to be leashed anyway. It would keep him and Francis out of trouble. I thought about turning the guy with the gun in to the soup kitchen director, but Marty said I was just asking for it if I did.

"He won't do anything at the kitchen. He likes it there, and he wouldn't do something that would get him kicked out. If you turn him in and he finds out, though, that's a different story. He's seen me and Francis over here. He'd put two and two together real fast and you'd be in danger."

The Friday afternoon of Memorial Day weekend, I opened my front door to head over to the soup kitchen and tripped over

Francis. He looked up at me, rolled over for me to rub his stomach, and gave me one of his by now infamous kisses. I looked around for Marty and saw him standing by himself next to the kitchen door. I smiled and waved. He returned both gestures. I gave Francis one last scratch behind his ears before going over to the church.

After dinner, Marty and I headed across my yard to the porch. Marty had taken to waiting outside the back door of the kitchen and walking over with me. He didn't think it looked good for him to be loitering on my porch alone. I knew almost immediately that something was wrong. Normally, as soon as Francis heard our voices, his large white face would appear above the ledge of the porch. He'd cock his head to the side and watch us with a restrained excitement that caused him to pant and tremble. My first thought was that he'd wandered off. Marty must have realized the situation as quickly as I did, because before I knew it we were both calling out his name. We looked up and down the street, in the backyard, in my neighbors' yards. Nothing. Finally, we went to the porch, figuring we'd collect our thoughts and come up with our next move. That's when we found Francis. He was stretched out on the welcome mat. At first, it appeared he was sleeping, but when Marty called for him and he didn't move, we both knew. Marty knelt down beside him, reached out and stroked his lifeless head. Suddenly, a horrible sound, a cross between a scream and a wail, erupted from the depths of my heart. I collapsed in my rocker, the sobs coming so hard that I could barely breathe. Marty just kept petting Francis.

"Are you all right?" I looked up and vaguely made out the shape of a person standing on the top step of my porch. He was a big man and he was wearing a jacket. "I heard all the racket and thought I'd better see if everything was okay."

Before I could answer, I heard a low growl. My first thought was that maybe Francis was still alive, but then I realized the sound was coming from Marty. He stood up and rounded on the man. His voice was barely above a whisper, but the fury behind it was palpable. "You shot my dog. You rotten son-of-a-bitch. I'll kill you, I swear I will."

I looked down at Francis and that's when I saw it — the small hole in the top of his head. The fur around it was tinged pink. I'd seen that kind of wound before. I'd come home that day from lunch with a friend and bent down to kiss Harley on the top of his head, thinking he was napping in his worn out recliner, only to discover the dried blood in his graying hair.

I heard the footsteps as Marty ran past me — felt his anger vibrate through the wooden boards of the porch floor. In an instant, he had the man with the jacket pinned to the ground, his hands around his captive's throat. The man struggled to free himself, and I thought of the gun I was sure he had stashed in one of his pockets.

"Hey, you two! Break it up!" Jack from across the street , a retired state policeman turned mall security guard, was running toward the fighting men. He pulled Marty off and sat him down on the bottom step. The other man rolled over on his side, gasping for breath. "What in hell is going on over here?"

Marty never looked up. "Son-of-a-bitch shot my dog."

I watched as Jack's gaze went from Marty to Francis to the choking man on my lawn. "Is that true, Mister?"

"Crazy . . . jerk . . . attacked me . . . for nothing."

"He's got a gun. He always carries a gun."

Jack's body tensed. His hand instinctively reached for the revolver hanging at his side. He trained the barrel on the dark-haired man sprawled on the ground. "I've already called in a disturbance, so someone will be here any minute. Until then, you'd best lay real still."

The police came and arrested the big man with the jacket for possession of a concealed weapon. I told Jack what had happened and he persuaded the officers not to arrest Marty. Once the squad cars left and Jack was once again on his side of the street, Marty picked up Francis' body and turned to leave.

"Where will you take him?" I asked.

"Don't know for sure." He buried his face in his friend's soft white fur and, with muffled moans, the tears finally came.

I laid my hand on his trembling shoulder. "How about here? I've got a big backyard where he could rest peaceful."

Marty looked up, thought for a moment and said, "I think Francis would like that. He sure liked you."

We buried Francis down by my butterfly garden beside a statue of his namesake.

For the next year or so, Marty would come to the soup kitchen on Friday nights and then he and I would pay Francis a visit. But, eventually Marty stopped coming and I lost contact with him. Whenever I looked out my dining room window at the butterfly garden, I'd remember our time together and say a prayer for my friend.

One day, Jack knocked on my door. He had heard from one of his police buddies that a homeless man had died over the weekend, so he'd gone down to the morgue to see if it was Marty. I knew from the look on his face that it was. I contacted Dignity Memorial Network, an organization for homeless and indigent veterans, and they paid for all the funeral expenses. I know it sounds trite, but I find comfort in the belief that Marty, Harley, and Francis are in a place where the nightmares are gone and no one is mean to them because of fear or prejudice. There are people who think death is the worst thing that can happen to a person, but that's not true. Living can be a lot worse.

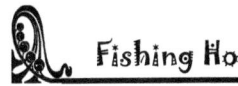

Fishing Holiday

Jeannine Baumgartle

We are all in the kitchen, in various stages of getting breakfast.

"What do you say we head for the lake this weekend?" my husband sings out, bubbling over with enthusiasm.

I should have anticipated something like this. A three-day weekend is coming up and for him; liberation is open air — wet, dry, cold, hot, whatever the season offers.

Four little voices toss hoorays in the air and dance around the room as if their Rice Krispies had caffeine. –Baby girl doesn't really get it, but bounces enthusiastically. When you're two, three older brothers can't be wrong — very often, anyway.

"Yay!" I submit. If she can catch the fun in her dimples, it's worth a try for me, as well. My smile performs around a stifled sigh.

A check-list forms in my mind of all the food we will need, clothing, first-aid kit, dog food, sun block, cell phones, bikes, a call to the church so they can find another nursery attendant, and one to our next-door neighbor so someone will know where we've gone (and keep an eye on things), all of the packing dependent upon the absolute necessity of cleaning out the camper.

The kids are *so* good the evening before we leave, not wanting to jeopardize the trip or frustrate the parents who will be granting favors along the way. Not that they aren't genuinely blissful!

We actually get underway early. I am the last one in the van, the approbation tentative among all the seat-belted countenances, if you can seat-belt a countenance. The trip there is easy — easy chatter, snacks, breaks. I know where my children are, feel they are getting the hang of traveling, beginning to know each other, and us.

I am bracing myself for the sudden escape from safety-belts to the water's edge.

#

The world is a kaleidoscope of experiences to our little group. I hadn't realized how much the children have grown since we were here last. No one is in diapers anymore. Even baby girl can drink out of a cup. My littlest guy climbs aboard the aging bass boat, expecting to try his hand at fishing. The older two can already manage, somewhat, so he will pretty much have his dad's full attention.

Pink Socks (baby girl) sees the boat slowly drifting away, and sets up a rumpus. Her dad catches this, holds out his arms to her (a signal to me) to bring her aboard. They wait where they are for me to wade into the cold water, which is too deep for baby girl, who pines for them all the way. I manage to plop her into her daddy's lap, and haul myself in as well. If I want any fishing to happen for the boys, someone will have to watch Pink Socks, that's for sure. So the six of us set off, grins in place, on the high seas.

In fifteen minutes, little girl is bored. No one wants to play. The guys are all involved with baiting hooks, and shoo her away every time she comes close to them.

"Want a drink, honey?" I ask. "How about a cookie?"

"Yes," she admits, without moving.

"We'll have to go back to the camper. . . ."

Reluctantly, little gal climbs on my back, and I prepare to slip over the side. She doesn't like the look of the water we're descending into, yells "Stop!", at the same time latching onto the side of the boat, throwing me off balance so that I lose my grip, and go under. A small bundle of mermaid plops onto me as I flail around, trying to get to my feet and get both of us some air.

"Everyone okay?" her dad calls out as we surface.

"Wonderful," I yell back, and that pretty well cures us girls of boating for the rest of the day. We play in the sand and wash off shells.

⊞ ⊞ ⊞

All in all, we have a good supper. The daddy cleans and filets the fish, the mother cooks the fish, and the children help them eat the fish. Barkley, our dog, has dogfood and a couple of treats. The boys put out the fire (don't ask how).

Later, after bike rides and a snack, we call it a night. The camper is predictably stuffy with the six of us and the dog. Our middle boy crawls over his siblings and taps his dad on the shoulder.

"Can we sleep outside?" he whispers. "It's hot in here, and Barkley doesn't smell so good."

"Let's do it," his dad agrees. He's been lying awake for some time, and sounds glad to get up. Gathering pillows and sleeping bags, trying to be quiet and in the process waking both brothers, they manage to climb out and choose a spot in the sandy grass. Barkely goes too, thank goodness. After a couple of minutes, my husband comes back in for a flashlight and some insect repellent. I clonk back to sleep immediately.

Later, when all the iced tea I've drunk catches up with me, I groan, and make myself get up. The camper door is standing open. Not one nook or cranny inside holds a Baby Girl. I descend on the guys with a shriek, spitting out frantic instructions to spread out and find her before . . . before . . . just find her!

Her dad and I race off, the boys, plus Barkley, charged with staying together and searching the restrooms and playground, which are lighted.

After what seems like a nightmare of my future life, Baby Girl turns up, sitting on a strand of beach. She is picking shells out of the sand, rinsing them the way we did earlier, and holding them up to the moonlight. I have never seen her more content.

"There you are," I call to her gently, as if she has merely been in her play room at home. Heart attack number two subsides.

Our poor tired family turns in again, this time with the door latched and locked.

Dawn doesn't interrupt our sleeping in.

The children, of course, awake refreshed, ready to eat, and we're off again. During this day, number one son steps in poison ivy and my husband digs out the calamine lotion; we find a tick crawling on son number two, but of course dispose of it before it can set up house-keeping. Son number three rides on his dad's shoulders as they walk down the beach, both of them looking a little sun-burned when they get back, in places both were exposed. You can see how they fit together, pale for pale, burn for burn.

At last, the calming down part of the trip for me: driving home, able to account for everyone and everything, except for one ball cap which is probably in a tree out there.

Monday is catch-up time. I do laundry for two days, losing count after about twelve loads; put another couple of hundred dollar's worth of gas in the camper, and remove all garbage and food-stuffs that might spoil. Restock on band-aids and calamine without losing a beat of our regular routine. No one falls overboard, or disappears in the night, or requires bug spray or calamine lotion.

Now *this* is my kind of a holiday.

Lonnie, Me and the Battle of St. Crispin's Day

Marian Allen

It all started when Lonnie got on Facebook. One minute, me and him were chuckling at his wife, Leona, and my wife, Mary Lee, for being "Face-heads", and the next minute, he's on there himself.

Not that he told me. The first I knew of it, Mary Lee whooped, "Oh! I don't believe it!" from the little room where she keeps the computer and her sewing machine. Then she stood in the doorway like she was leaning on it for support and said, "Guess who just friended me."

"Lady Goo-goo."

"Lady Gaga, and no. Lonnie Carter."

"Lonnie Carter? Our Lonnie Carter? Across the street Lonnie Carter? What in the world is Lonnie doing on there?"

"Ask him yourself," she said. "He's on here now."

She ducked back into The Hole, waving to me to follow, but I'm built like a linebacker — maybe a little gone to seed — and no way would there be room in there for me, much less me and Mary Lee and a computer and a sewing machine. I grabbed my Bigman husky-plus jacket and hot-footed across the street.

Leona opened the back door before I knocked. When I asked her where Lonnie was, she grinned like a polecat and pointed toward the living room.

And there he sat, holding some kind of little something in his long skinny knobby hand and poking at it with one finger, looking as serious as if he was working.

"Hey, buddy," I said.

He jumped so hard, the thing flew up out of his hands and tumbled through the air. He snatched at it but missed and the thing landed plump on the couch cushion beside him.

"Dang it, Tiny!" He grabbed the thing and rubbernecked between inspecting it for damage and glaring up at me. "I coulda broke my smart phone!"

I would have thought giving Lonnie Carter a smart phone was about like giving a banana to a cat, but he sat me down and showed it off and seemed to know how to work it.

"And you know," he said, "you and me has had some laughs about this Facebook thing, but Leona got me onto it and who do you think friended me?"

"Lady Goo-ga."

Leona came in with a cup of coffee for each of us, said, "Lady Goo-ga?" and went back into the kitchen.

I gave up. "Well, who was it?"

"Daniel Halloran."

"Daniel. . . . Daniel. . . ." The name was ringing a bell, somewhere in there. "Danny Halloran? Dime-Store Danny? King of the Five-Finger Discount?"

"That's the one! And guess what he's doing?"

"Ten to twenty for grand larceny?"

"No, he's a priest! Father Dan is what they call him. And guess where he's priesting?"

Lonnie r'ared back on the couch and bobbed his head in encouragement, but I was all done guessing for the day. "I don't know, Lonnie. Tell me."

"Saints Crispin and Crispinian. And guess what day it's getting to be."

It was a day I hadn't thought of for over twenty years, but Lonnie had harked me back, and I knew right away what he meant.

"St. Crispin's Day," I said.

If you have a Catholic church in your neighborhood — at least, if you had one when Lonnie and me were growing up — and if it was named after a saint, you had a festival on or around that saint's day every year. Saints Crispin and Crispinian, being twins, had the same feast day, but everybody just called it St. Crispin's Day for short.

"And Danny invited us back."

"Say what?"

"St. Crispin's Day, Tiny. October 25. The festival's this Saturday."

#

So the next thing I know, I'm heading across town, back to the old neighborhood, with Lonnie running off at the mouth about stuff I'd just as soon forget. The only good thing was that Mary Lee wasn't there to hear some of it.

"Happy days," Lonnie kept saying. "Good days."

It made my hair stand on end.

"How'd you talk Leona into letting you off the leash?" Not that Mary Lee and me have some kind of open marriage or anything, but Leona keeps a sharper eye on Lonnie than Mary Lee does on me. In fact, Mary Lee says the only thing about me that gives her any cause for concern is hanging around with Lonnie. But that's just talk. Her and Leona live in each other's pockets; it would break either one of them's heart if Lonnie and me stopped being friends.

Lonnie winked in answer to my question and said, "Trust ol' Lonnie." He patted my shoulder, like that would reassure me. I figured what he meant was, Leona was counting on me to keep him out of trouble. From the way he had one ankle crossed over his knee, foot wiggling, fingers twiddling on his legs, it looked like I was going to have my day cut out for me.

Before I knew it, we were driving along streets that looked kind of familiar but no kind of familiar. A lot of houses and businesses were exactly where and how I remembered, but some were missing, some were wrecks, some had siding instead of the wood they were born with. Some trees were bigger than I remembered, and some were stumps. Lena's grocery had a big BODEGA sign on it and the window in the side of the building where we used to line up for snow-cones said "fruteria" over it.

Sts. Crispin and Crispinian hadn't changed, though. Still big and Gothic in the front, with brick additions straggling out behind it. The street that ran in front of it was barricaded off for two blocks in either direction for the festival.

"I was forgetting about that," I said. The last time we were around for St. Crispin's Day, neither one of us could drive, not to mention that we could walk to it from where we lived.

Lonnie pulled out that phone of his and started giving me directions.

"How does that thing know how to go?"

"It's got a map on it, see?"

After I didn't hit a lamppost and a garbage can while Lonnie had his phone up my nose, I followed his directions and got around the blockade and into the rectory parking lot.

Lonnie did a few more beeps and boops on his phone and unfolded his long skinny self out of my car.

I reached up and picked a dry brown catalpa pod off the tree above us.

"Remember the time we tried smoking these things?"

A big voice boomed, "I prefer cigars these days, and I'm trying to cut down on those."

The big voice belonged to a tubby priest with a round red nose, bright blue eyes and thinning strawberry blond hair.

If Lonnie hadn't told me who we were meeting, I would never have known him.

"Danny? Dang, Dime-Store! Long time!"

"Tiny! Weasel!"

We wrung each other's hands and slapped each other's shoulders and stood around laughing with our hands in our pockets until a thin old woman opened the back door.

"Tea's getting cold, Father Dan."

We followed Danny through the kitchen and down a hall into a cluttered and comfortable sitting room that might have belonged to any normal bachelor. Well, except that there was a tray on the coffee table with a teapot on it, and tea cups and a bowl of sugar lumps and a tray of cookies.

When the old lady had closed the door behind herself, Lonnie put on a high voice and said, "May I have two lumps of sugar, Miss Halloran?"

Danny shook a fist and said, "Two lumps upside the head, Weasel!"

"Folks don't call me that no more, Dime-Store. I'm just plain Lonnie, now."

"Folks don't call me Dime-Store, either, you know."

Lonnie said, "Naw, it's *Father* Dime-Store, these days."

"I'm still Tiny," I said, and they both laughed.

Danny reached around to a cabinet behind his chair and pulled out a bottle of Beam. He tipped some into his own cup and held the open neck toward ours. "Touch of Kentucky?"

"I married me a hard-shell Baptist," Lonnie said. Then he winked and said, "But what the little woman don't know won't hurt me."

I waved the bottle off. Not that I don't drink — I just don't like whiskey.

"I'm saving myself for the beer garden," I said. "You do still have a beer garden, don't you?"

That set Lonnie back off on the "happy days" magical memory tour about how us boys would sneak into the festival's beer garden and drink the leftovers and get sick. Yeah, I really wanted to relive those moments. It's a wonder we didn't catch AIDS or diphtheria or something.

After we finished the tea and whatnot, Danny led us on through the rectory and out the front door, down the walk and out the gate and maybe twenty years back in time.

There were a lot of new faces, and a lot of older faces that used to be younger. Everybody who remembered us was glad to see us — or pretended they were, anyway. Our old friends' mothers seemed to get a charge out of telling us how great their kids were doing now, implying that our moving out of the neighborhood was the best thing that ever happened to it.

All the games were the same. They called the bean bag toss "corn hole" now, for some reason, but it was the same game. Looked like the same equipment, come to that.

Danny strutted around with us, waving at parishioners, laughing at our friends' mothers' jokes about the shines we used to get up to. It didn't take me long to have enough, and I would have been just as happy to go on home, but Lonnie was having a blast, and I didn't have the heart to throw a wet blanket on him.

When we got to the beer garden, I decided not to get a beer, after all. I was hoping to be driving home sooner rather than later, and I had perfectly good beer in my own refrigerator. I reminded Lonnie he was going to be breathing at Leona by and by, and Danny backed me up, so we all three got bratwurst and lemon slush and sat down at a picnic table to take in the passing show.

I'd finished my brat and half my slush when I heard a sound that made my blood run cold: Lonnie giggled. Not just one giggle, like a little burp that surprises you when you swallow water too fast. No, this was a giggle fit that meant something, like belching "America the Beautiful" on a bet. I swiveled around toward him, and there he was, red in the face, covering his mouth and giggling, tears of laughter squeezed out of the corners of his eyes, and that damned Danny grinning like the cat that ate the canary.

"You didn't," I said. "You did. You underhanded mackerel-snapper; you been spiking his slush for him, haven't you?"

"Oh, what's the harm? You're driving, and I didn't slip it to him unaware — just offered it and poured it where it was wanted."

"Like Lonnie's got any sense."

Danny had the grace to look a little doubtful.

"Well, let's get him back to the rectory, and run some cold water over his head and pour some straight black coffee down him."

I talked Lonnie into eating his brat first, and that steadied him some. Danny probably hadn't given him all that much, but he wasn't used to anything but the (very) occasional beer, and he probably felt drunker than he was. He walked okay, talked just a little louder than usual, and thought everything he'd already seen on the way to the beer garden was surprising and wonderful on the way back.

He dug a fold of ones out of his pocket and played every game of chance we passed except the cakewalk. I'd talk him out of playing, then I'd get buttonholed by some hen who'd known my Mom and, when I looked around, Lonnie would be at another one. He won a stuffed panda at the Wheel O' Chance, which he seemed to think Leona would like.

We almost made it. We were right there at the rectory gate when somebody opened the door to the parish hall and a burst of music came out.

"Dancing!" Lonnie shouted. He faked a little tap routine. "Gotta dance! Gotta dance!" He tossed the panda into my arms and loped away from us.

Drinking and gambling and dancing. Leona was purely gonna kill me!

I'm big, but I'm not that fast, and Father Dan couldn't but waddle. By the time we got into the hall, Lonnie had worked his way into the crowd and cut in on a guy who didn't look all too happy about it. The woman he was dancing with was laughing.

I recognized her. Then I recognized the guy.

"Are you kidding me? He's in here two seconds, after twenty years away, and he zeroes in on Jackie the Kipper?" Jacob deKueper, his real name was, but he was "Jackie the Kipper" to us boys, and his big brother, Pete, was "Dutch".

Danny was sweating, and not just from the heat of the parish hall.

"I didn't realize the deKuepers would be here. I haven't seen any of them around for over five years. Jackie must have gotten time off for good behavior."

And the woman.

"Isn't that Yvonne Hargrove Lonnie cut in on?"

"Yvonne deKueper."

"She married the Kipper?"

"She married Dutch."

"This just gets better and better." I craned around, looking for somebody my size but uglier and meaner.

"Surely Dutch won't be here." Danny ran a finger around the inside of his dog collar, then made a twitchy gesture that looked an awful like an unconscious sign of the cross. "Dutch is still wanted in the hold-up that got Jackie put away."

"I'm gonna go peel Lonnie off that handful of trouble he's dancing with and get going. Thanks for the good time, old pal. If I ever invite you over to my place, take my advice and don't come."

"Sorry, Tiny." His voice faded behind me as I plowed through the dancers.

"Lonnie. . . . Lonnie. . . . Hi, there, Yvonne. Congratulations on your marriage to Dutch."

Lonnie, snockered as he was, let go of her like she'd just grown porcupine spines.

"Dutch? Where? Where's Dutch?"

You know how, in a movie, when somebody asks a question like that, everything gets real quiet, and then you hear an ominous voice saying something like, "He's right here," or "Look behind you," or "Who wants to know?"

Well, Lonnie asked where was Dutch, and then he staggered back and sprawled on the floor and the world in front of me was filled with a fist.

I'd know that right anywhere. Those knuckles fit up against my left eye like they were coming home. Somehow, I'd known Dutch would have grown as much as I had, and my automatic return punch tagged him right where I meant to: above his left eye. Opened the skin of his brow. Didn't do any real damage, but Jackie was, sure enough, still squeamish at the sight of blood, so there was one of Dutch's allies out of commission.

Like always, Dutch hadn't come alone, and one of his cronies picked Lonnie up and threw him toward another guy's fist. Lonnie's legs wouldn't hold him, though, and he reeled out of range.

Women screamed, men shouted, and more than a few folks, overexcited by what Leona would have called the twin devils of drink and dance music, chose up sides and took the opportunity to settle some scores of their own that didn't have thing one to do with Dutch or Lonnie or me.

One bad thing about being big which you might never have thought of, unless you're big, yourself, is that you're kind of hard to miss. Not only can people see you, they can throw a punch in a pretty general direction and still land a hit. And being big doesn't mean a punch doesn't hurt you as much as it hurts a little guy, either.

I'd like to say I gave as good as I got, but I wasn't exactly keeping score. All I can say is, my hands hurt about as much as all the rest of me, so I must have been tagging somebody. At first, it was just my right hand that hurt, and then I realized I was still holding that damn panda. I tried using it for a shield, but Dutch and his boys didn't have a sentimental bone in all their bodies, and they didn't mind punching a stuffed panda any more than they did a person. Then I tried lambasting guys with it, but it didn't even slow them down. By and by, I lost hold of it and it went I knew not where.

All the time, I kept half an ear out for sirens. In my younger days, which I should have remembered, the festival wasn't complete without at least one fistfight breaking out somewhere, though things didn't usually get as general as this one seemed to be. The cops ought to be on the alert, although times had gotten rougher and maybe a mere knock-down drag-out didn't rate anymore.

I could hear Danny's voice, amplified by the sound system, saying, "Boys! Boys! . . . And ladies! A saint's day is no time for violence! Think of the children!" but no sirens.

After what seemed like about three years, when I was backed up against the bingo tables that had been shoved up along the walls, I gave Dutch a good solid wallop and he didn't come back.

Something tugged at my jeans so hard I was afraid my pants would come off, so I took the advice my legs had been giving me for some time and sat down.

"Scrootch on under here, buddy," Lonnie whispered.

I scrootched on under, and there was Lonnie, without a mark on him, with that phone of his out and him beeping and booping on it to beat the band.

"Lonnie," I said, "what in the ever-lovin' blue-eyed world are you doing?"

"Tweeting with Plaid Girl and L. R. Lee," he said, like that ought to make sense. "They think you're doing great. She said she's going to write you a haiku, and he said for me to take some pictures for him, since he can't be here to take 'em hisself."

"Do I know these people?"

"No."

"Do you know these people?"

"Well, sure."

"I mean in real life."

"Tiny, you just don't get it, do you?"

I figured I'd already got about as much as I could handle. "I guess I don't," I said. "Why don't you just hold onto it for me and I'll get it by and by."

Things sounded like they were sorting themselves out in the world beyond the tables. Danny told everybody to clear the hall until they'd cleaned up and cooled down.

Once everything was nice and quiet, we crawled out from under the tables. Time teaches wisdom, my mama used to say, and it looked like there was some truth to it. The parish hall hadn't been decorated at all, and the bingo tables up against the walls had kept flying fists and feet and people out of the windows. The floor was littered with paper and neckties and ball caps and maybe the occasional tooth, but nothing more valuable than that.

"Time to go, buddy," I said.

I almost had him out when he said, "Leona's prize!" We scrounged around and he found it up on the stage, stuffing popping out of its seams and one of its eyes hanging by a thread but, amazingly, no blood on it.

"Somebody's went and blacked both its poor ol' eyes," Lonnie mourned.

"It's a panda, Lon. It comes with black eyes."

I would have told him to leave it but I figured with one hand full of panda and the other full of phone, he couldn't drink anything or play anything or grab ahold of anything, so I let it be.

We left by the back door, heading for the rectory parking lot.

Speaking of two black eyes, by the time we got to the car, both mine were just about swollen shut. I wasn't about to ride in any car Lonnie was driving, with him full of whiskey slush and still plaiding or twitting or whatever he was doing with that damn phone.

But the last sight I saw before my eyes hurt too much to hold them open was Mary Lee, arms crossed, leaning against the driver's-side door.

#

It was a swift and silent ride home. Mary Lee drives like she's getting paid for it — not a second wasted, just barely legal. Every time Lonnie started to say something, she said, "No," or, "Hush up," or, "Don't talk or I'll slaughter you." She didn't tell him he couldn't beedledy-boop on his phone, though, so there was quite a bit of that.

Leona was waiting for us at our house. Lonnie tucked the phone away and, sliding out of Mary Lee's reach, said, "Honey, I—"

"We'll talk about it at home, you back-sliding reprobate," she said. "Go on and mix yourself up a Alka-Seltzer before you get sick. I'll be right behind you."

"I brung you something." He held out that raggedy-butt panda and waggled it so the loose eye flapped around.

"I know," she said. "Won it in a game of chance, didn't you? Didn't you?"

Lonnie turned the bear around and looked at it like it was going to give him the answer.

"Home," Leona said.

Lonnie shuffled off home, saying, "C'mon, Chance. You and me is in the doghouse. Ain't you ashamed of yourself, fighting and all?"

"Leona," I said, "I am so sorry."

"You done your best," she said. She gave me a quick hug and a pat on the shoulder and hugged Mary Lee real big and sniffled.

"Mary Lee," she said, "you two are the best friends ever. I thank the Lord for the both of you." She sniffled again and left.

Mary Lee led me into the kitchen and sat me down. I heard the freezer open and shut and she handed me two bags of frozen peas to hold against my eyes. She put some coffee to brew and sat down across the table from me.

One good thing I'll say about having a friend like Lonnie: Whenever you get in trouble, folks always assume it's his fault. Of course, one bad thing about having a friend like Lonnie is: it usually is his fault.

Mary Lee said, "'These wounds I had on Crispin's day.' Remember? That battle speech in Henry V that you did in Senior English?"

I hadn't remembered it, but now I did. "Did he win? Ol' King Henry?"

"Yes. 'He to-day that sheds his blood with me shall be my brother; be he ne'er so vile.'"

"Is that a fact?"

"You don't remember?"

I said, "I was lucky to remember it long enough to recite it in Senior English." Then I said, "How did you know I needed you? Have we been married that long?"

"I knew because that fool was updating his status on Facebook the whole time. He knows Leona and I are on there. He knows we get his status updates. And yet there he was, posting pictures and going, 'Danny slips me a little Kentucky while Tiny isn't looking. Ha-ha,' and 'Tiny don't want me to have no fun, but I'm a growed man and I know a trick or two.'"

The sheer stupidity of it made me dizzy.

"And then the fight started, and he crawled under some tables and stuck the phone up and snapped pictures and videos. People were rooting for you and sharing the pictures and—" She got up and got us each a cup of coffee.

I took the peas off my eyes and found I could open my peepers enough to see her sweet face.

She said, "Leona was beside herself, so I got Bernadette to run me in and drop me off." Bernadette was the little old lady who lived next door. Feisty little firecracker — I was half-way surprised she didn't wade into the fight instead of just dropping Mary Lee off. She must have had a hair appointment.

The fight was on the local news, and it seems that the guy who pulled Dutch off of me was the cop working the hold-up Dutch was wanted for. The cops had turned up, after all, but they hadn't used their sirens because they didn't want to scare Dutch off.

I called Lonnie — on the regular phone — and Leona let him talk, once she found out it was me calling.

"I'm glad you at least had the sense to call the police with that play-toy of yours."

"I didn't call the police. A man don't call the police to settle his fights for him."

I didn't say it, but I thought, "No, a man crawls under the bingo tables and lets another man settle 'em."

"Naw," Lonnie said. "Somebody on Facebook seen the pictures I took that had saw Dutch on Local Most Wanted, and they called the cops. I ain't no stool pigeon."

"G'night, Lonnie," I said, and hung up the phone real gentle. I went and sat back down next to Mary Lee. "'Ne'er so vile,' huh?" I said. "You know, sometimes I wonder what I see in him, myself."

Trick or Treat Night

Jeannine Baumgartle

So silly, for me,
a grown woman, to
yearn for Halloween.
All those childish dress-ups,
the secret identity we used to carry
to people's doors, in any weather—
a rite of passage, it was,
rewarded with candy.
I still have the sweet tooth,
(or maybe insecurities
that need to be fed)
sweep the walk in moonlight
as though seeking a lost self;
lock the door only after the candle
has burned all the way down.

Feast of the Dead
Ardis Moonlight

It was unusual for our family to be in Florida at the end of October. Normally the visits were made in the summer when we could swim in the Gulf. Or we'd come down at Christmas to visit Mom's mother who lived in St. Pete.

This year was very different because Dad's brother had died in July. We didn't make our usual trip in the summer, but Mom decided a trip to Siesta Key, one of the small islands off the coast of the town of Sarasota, would help us all, especially Dad who was really grieving.

Once we got to the motel where we always stayed, Dad would go through the motions of day-to-day living, but he didn't laugh or smile. I wished there was something I could say or do to change that for him or even the sadness I felt.

I remember just last year when Uncle Harry visited us. He and Dad laughed about their childhood nicknames for each other — both had loved Latin and animals. Uncle Harry's was Felis, which is the first part of the scientific name for cat. Uncle Harry would sneak up on everyone then pounce on them, although Dad was his usual target. Dad would retaliate later by calling out like a screech owl, which is a very creepy sound, and scare Harry. So Dad's nickname was Otus, which is the first part of the scientific name for screech owl.

My sister Beth, who was 12, and I, two years older, liked being at the beach because it wasn't just us; there were several families from Ohio and New Jersey, and lots of teenagers, anywhere from pre-teen to 17. It gave us both opportunities to study the nuances of being a teen, something I was having difficulty getting. Flirting seemed so fake to me, yet all the girls from Ohio knew how to do it, and the boys loved it. So often I felt like I was in a foreign country and didn't understand the language at all.

One Ohio girl I was especially entranced by was Muriel, a cheerleader-type. She wore her thick brown hair in a ponytail, and had a smile that lit up her whole face. She could even make my Dad smile, which was something then. Muriel and I sometimes hung out together. I spent most of my time watching her, wishing I could be at ease with the boys, too.

Since it was the end of October, one of the older kids thought it'd be neat to have a Halloween party on the beach. My parents approved as long as we were home by 10:30; if we weren't, Dad would come get us. He had done that earlier in the week and called out to us from afar with the flashlight shining on the group; at least he hadn't walked right up to everyone — I would have died.

All the teenagers were excited about the Halloween party. Muriel was going as a princess in a clingy top and gypsy-type skirt, hoop earrings, and a silver eye mask. Being a beach bum suited me. I wore cut-off jeans, a ripped-up green tee shirt my dad was pitching out, old tennis shoes, a green tie (also my dad's) around my head; the tie looked like seaweed, if you used your imagination. I even created scars on my face and neck with makeup crayons. Beth went as a cat — with crayoned whiskers, cut-out cardboard ears attached to a head band, and a black shirt and cut-offs. Her tail was a brown scarf pinned together and stuffed with toilet paper — no one had a solid black scarf.

The ocean was rough that night, which wasn't a surprise; it was October. The wind whistled across the sand and through the pines along the edge of the beach. But the stars were out in abundance, and the quarter moon would be up around 10.

I didn't recognize anyone that night except for Muriel, Beth, and Jim, Muriel's new friend. About 20 kids, costumed as clowns, witches, ghosts, pirates, and gypsies, ebbed and flowed around the potato chips, cheese and crackers, orange slices, cookies, and soft drinks. The flickering light from a fire in a small metal can tucked into the sand distorted the features of anyone passing by.

Someone brought a radio. Beth and I watched the wild gyrations of those who chose to dance on the beach, but mostly we watched Muriel and Jim.

Jim, a 16-year-old from New Jersey, had been hanging around Muriel a lot. He was cute, had short, curly brown hair, and was a magician with his cape. He did magic tricks like the coin stuff where it'd disappear in his hand and he'd retrieve it from your ear, or toss it in the air, and find it on Muriel's arm or in my seaweed tie.

When the music abruptly ended; everyone stopped moving. A witch stood by the fire and called out, "Come join me to celebrate this night. You know it as Halloween, but it's a very old celebration. It was once called the Feast of the Dead."

That brought us to her. The light flickered across a face with warts and wrinkles, and she stared at us with deep dark eyes, looking very old and wise. Everyone settled themselves on the sand and listened.

In a deep voice with the wind whistling around her, she continued, "On this night, there is a crack between this world and the world of the dead. So they return, the ghosts we know and love, to their families and friends. For, you see, these families would have a special feast honoring their ghostly guests. And sometimes the dead would bring advice to help the living. Tonight, when you return to your homes, remember your own ghosts. Celebrate their lives. Learn that death is nothing to fear!" She tossed something in the flame, which smoked then flared, which made us gasp. The eerie music of "Night on Bald Mountain" tugged at the dark and crept around the gathering. The witch waved a broom, motioning us to follow her as she began a dance on the sand. First, the ghosts joined, and gradually, we all linked hands and followed her movements around the beach. At times, I thought I saw shimmers of others not in costume moving in and around us. Was Uncle Harry here?

Eventually the eerie music stopped; a rock and roll piece played in its place, changing the atmosphere. The party felt over for me. I whispered to Beth, who had been next to me throughout the death dance, "I'm ready to go."

"Me, too."

Muriel and Jim were nearby. I told them we were leaving.

"Hey, Jim and I will walk you back and protect you from ghosts," she said grinning.

After we crossed the road that ran by the beach and pine trees, we followed the sandy lane until we reached the "jungle", which was a stretch of palm trees, palmettos, and large-leaved foliage that didn't let in much light during the day and barely anything at night. It took up more than a block and was about 20 feet wide. As younger kids, we imagined this was home for snakes, panthers, enormous spiders, huge lizards, as well as plants that could swallow us whole. Although we knew most of that was impossible, being older, the jungle still could scare us.

We would have taken the lane around the towering stretch of darkness, but Jim stepped forward. "I'll lead the way," he said and reached for Muriel's hand. She reached for mine; I held Beth's. Just as we started into the jungle, Muriel moved my hand into Jim's and slipped away. Thinking that was weird, I just decided to savor holding a boy's hand for the first time. After a few minutes of walking, Jim glanced back, saying, "I'll protect you. . . ." Realizing I wasn't Muriel, he dropped my hand and ran back to where we entered.

I felt hurt, but Beth whispered, "Muriel's playing a mean trick on you. Let's keep going."

I was startled. Beth sometimes seemed so much wiser than I. We walked softly and slowly, just in case our childish imaginings were real, although the thoughts of ghosts blotted out the jungle scare. When we were halfway through, I whispered, "Let's hide so they don't know where we are."

We crept behind some of the palmetto, and waited.

"Muriel, where are you?" Jim called outside the jungle.

I whispered, "I thought she'd be out there laughing."

"Me, too."

"Muriel, this isn't funny. Where are you?" Jim called. Quiet. He screamed.

Beth and I waited in the silence, which seemed forever. Muriel called out at the other end of the jungle. "Maggie! Beth! Are you in there? Something's happened to Jim."

We didn't say anything. Beth squeezed my hand.

"Maggie. Beth. Please answer. I need help."

Beth whispered, "Where is he hiding?"

"I don't know."

It was easy to be quiet; we were both scared, and I was still thinking about the Feast of the Dead and Uncle Harry. Glimmers of moonlight made the jungle spooky. The rustles nearly and overhead didn't help.

"Do you still think they're hiding in there?" Jim said.

"They can't be. Everybody's scared of this place."

"I'll bet they went back the other way."

"We'd have seen them."

"It was too dark. Come on, let's go back to the beach."

Beth whispered, "Let's scare them."

We moved quietly to where we had walked in and listened as Muriel and Jim's steps scuffled in the sand as they came closer to us. "You really think they went home?"

"Yeah, I think they tore out of there right after me. I heard lots of noises behind me before I found you."

They heard the sound when we did. A slow wailing that built, then echoed in the night. I clutched Beth's hand and closed my eyes. Muriel screamed. We watched as they ran to the beach. Jim's cape seemed to fly.

The wail came again, flowing out and over us. "Is that Dad?" Beth whispered.

"Dad?"

"Otus! It's the screech owl call!"

I was afraid to move. "You think Dad's in the tree?"

"No. It's a real screech owl."

We looked up in tree over us, but didn't see any owls, however, screech owls are so small. Something much larger was edging along the heaviest branch. A deep ghostly moan stirred the leaves, and golden eyes stared down at us.

Beth and I ran as fast as we could to the end of the sandy road, and back to the motel. We kept hearing sounds behind us.

Neither of us slept well that night. When we gathered for breakfast, I looked at Mom and then Dad, who seemed a little different. I told them about the Feast of the Dead and what happened in the jungle.

Dad's eyes got all shiny when I finished. "I need to tell you the dream I had last night. I was walking on a sandy path in a very large jungle — it was dark in places with all the foliage. A large black panther with golden eyes moved slowly out into the path and moaned softly. I said, 'Felis? Is that you?' The panther brushed his head against me then lunged up and placed his large paws on my shoulders. I was crying, and he licked away my tears, then dropped to the path and began walking away. I suddenly leaped on a small branch — I had become a screech owl; I called out. Felis turned around and roared. We both laughed and laughed, and the dream ended."

Dad cried, and Mom moved over and hugged him tightly. Beth and I sat there looking at each other, our eyes very large.

The next year, our family began the tradition of celebrating the Feast of the Dead. Beth and I still do.

Goldie
Marian Allen

"Help yourself to anything in the garden," Moira said, wrapping her thick black hair up in a paisley turban. "Leave the stuff on the mantle alone."

There was nothing of interest on the mantle, Larsen discovered, when Moira had pulled out of the driveway. Some candles, a brass bowl on a pedestal foot, and a switch (probably for getting fire from the fireplace to light the candles, he decided).

Absently carrying the switch with him, he checked out the raised-bed garden. Too bad Alicia couldn't come house-sitting with him. . . . He was lonely. . . . He scraped the switch along the roundness of a full-bodied pumpkin, then tapped it once . . . twice . . . a third time.

The pumpkin disappeared and a woman stood before him — Young, lovely, luscious, with tawny skin and amber eyes, hair short and smooth and orange except for that one perky green cowlick in the center.

"Hi," she said, in a rich contralto. She was ripe and ready and they were in bed before you could say, "Bibbidy-bobbidy-boo."

Goldie, he called her. She didn't call him anything. She was a girl of few words.

After several hours, Larsen asked if she was hungry.

"Moira fed me before she left," Goldie said, "but you have something, if you like."

Out of consideration for Goldie's feelings — assuming that she had any — Larsen fixed himself a cheeseburger without the bun or, of course, lettuce, tomato, or pickles.

After several more hours, Larsen fell into an exhausted slumber.

He woke alone.

"Goldie?" She wasn't in the bathroom. She wasn't in the living room.

"Goldie?" The kitchen door stood open. She wasn't on the deck. Footprints began at the bottom of the deck steps and proceeded down the beach.

"Goldie?" Larsen followed the footprints past two more beach houses, until the stars were blotted out by electric lights and the surf was muffled by juke-box music.

And there was Goldie, seated at an umbrella table at a beach-front dive. Seated on the lap of a leering blond man, rather. As Larsen watched, Goldie kissed the man wetly, then moved to the lap of another man, who pulled her close as she twined her arms around his neck. A third man massaged her back, and she arched her body and laughed.

"Goldie!" Larsen shouted.

She looked up, her round face silhouetted by the illuminated clock on the wall behind her. The clock's minute hand ticked forward to join the hour hand in standing straight up.

Midnight.

Without a flash or a puff of smoke, Goldie was gone, and a full-bodied pumpkin lay on the sand.

Larsen took it back to the house. He put it on the table, with the switch on one side of it and a butcher knife on the other. It was a long, long time before he made his choice.

He had thought she might make a pie but, in the end, she was nothing but a tart.

Flor de Muerto
Dirk Griffin

on these altars
veneration
expectation
communication

gifts are monuments
to loss and longing

speak in candlelight
the warmth of fire
removes the chill
and after this journey
from death to life
rest before
you must
at last
return

The Cautionary Tale of Silas Rockport
Marian Allen

Silas Rockport was the King of Thanksgiving. He began with Happy Thanksgiving Day cards (Traditional and Spiritual at first, followed by Contemporary and Humorous). Then, reasoning that atheists had no emotional investment in Thanksgiving, and vegetarians had no gustatory investment in Turkey Day, he instigated and funded a grass-roots campaign to conceptualize the celebration as Togetherness Day. He pushed it all over the world, as an exotic import from the swinging but oh-so-sentimental USA.

The Togetherness Day cards were a big hit, and so were the matching paper napkin/plate/tablecloth sets, hot-'n'-cold cups sold separately. He did a big business in fragile centerpieces that only lasted a couple of years, but a soul-less rival came up with fragile-looking plastic ones that were indestructible, and Silas lost most of his market share.

That was when he had his first brainstorm: edible centerpieces for Thanksgiving/Turkey/Togetherness Day. The centerpieces — no! the masterpieces! — were spun of irradiated vegetable matter (artificial color and flavoring added) and came in a variety of styles and prices. One of the most popular was Autumn Leaves, made of cranberry sauce (red), buttery mashed potatoes (pale gold), sweet potatoes (deep gold), turkey — marinated tofu for the vegetarians — (brown) and pumpkin pie (orange). The higher-priced model sat on a revolving music box which played "September Song," which wasn't very appropriate, title-wise, but was all about the autumn leaves, and nobody ever remembered the real title, anyway.

His second brainstorm came after he had read, with mounting fury, a series of grateful letters from satisfied customers, telling him that they loved his company's paper and plastic products so much they treated them gently, washed them carefully, and used them year after year with the pride of tradition. He knew that making a shoddier product would only alienate his market base, so they had him by the short hairs, there. Then it hit him — make the intended disposable products edible, too! He'd like to see them re-use something little Johnny had taken a great big slobbery bite out of!

The new items took off like wild turkeys. As the old paper and plastic goods eventually did wear out, the old customers bought into the new paradigm and, each year, the goods that weren't eaten were run through paper shredders and given to the dogs. "Just like at that First Glorious Get-Together!" dewy-eyed people in commercials said, as music swelled and they choked back their humble tears.

Next, he launched a line of Togetherness Day action figures: Pilgrims, Indians, log cabins, scale model of Plymouth Rock, rustic tables, loseable and replaceable plastic foods, deluxe set includes your choice of Pilgrim or Indian costume in S, M, L, or XL, specify boy or girl. A Saturday morning action-hero cartoon show naturally followed, with a muscular John Smith, an equally muscular Powhaton, and warrior-babe Pocahontas uniting to fight the forces of Evil throughout the universe. The movie broke sales records on its opening weekend.

All good things come to an end, even a life of success and riches. The time came when Silas Rockport stood before the judgment throne of God. He was a little nervous, but he subscribed to a faith that believed once saved, always saved, and he had been saved as a boy (he congratulated himself on his forethought) and wasn't really worried.

"I throw myself on Your mercy," he told God, smugly.

"We were afraid you might," said God. "So We've recused Ourself from your case."

". . .You've . . . what?"

"Recused Ourself. Your case will be tried in another court."

God's throne room faded like the metaphor it was, and was replaced by a room built of wood. Most of the room was filled with backless benches, shimmering under a press of barely-visible forms. At the back was a double door, closed and barred. At the front was a dais and a judge's bench big enough to seat seven. Figures glimmered and coalesced behind the bench, and seven men, dressed in somber blacks and browns, took their seats.

"Ladies and gentlemen," said the Voice of God, "from those same wonderful folks who gave you the Salem Witch Trials, We are proud to present — THE PURITANS."

Now, some think the Puritans had no sense of humor, but those people are mistaken. For example, take the judgment against Silas Rockport. His companies had made a packet for him on Wall Street, so they gave him the stocks. His cartoon show and spin-off movies were packed with simplistic violence, so they had him beaten with simple big thick sticks. He had invented, promoted, and commercialized Togetherness Day, so they tied his hands together, likewise his feet. They didn't strip him because, as one said, they always had liked the dressing as well as anything, and they sent him somewhere to roast until tender.

Considering what they had to work with, he would be a very long time in preparation, but they were Puritans, and they knew how to wait.

The Cautionary Tale of Silas Rockport originally appeared at Laughter Loaf.

Christmas Bizarre

Southern Indiana Writers

The Christmas Pool

Marian Allen

"So, are you interested? — Joy? — Ms. Crawford?"

Yes, I was interested, but the price set off alarm bells in my cynical mind. The house cost so little. . . It was a small house, but it came with ten acres of woods and a pool. Well, a pond, really, but the banks were steep except for one gentle shelf. Iris and cattails surrounded the pool and three koi — fat, pink, gold-dappled carp the size of dachshunds — lived in it.

"Does the pool freeze over in the winter?" I asked Carol Pittinger, the realtor/owner.

"Most years, thank God," she said.

Odd thing to say, I thought. I like ice skating as well as the next woman, which is why I had asked, but I didn't invoke the Deity over it.

I had the house inspected, of course, and I even had a check run on the pool, just to make sure there was nothing noxious about it. Those koi might have been dumped in for window dressing, for all I knew; they might die and be replaced daily. I had a dog to think of, after all.

Baxter Browning (my mutt) loved the place. He thought he'd died and gone to Sunnybank. "Look, Mom, I'm Lad! Look, I'm Bruce, the collie without a flaw!" I could almost hear him shouting.

"None of the above!" I shouted back, not caring if anyone heard me and thought I was a little cracked. I had long ago stopped caring what anyone else thought of me. It had been a hard dependence to break, but now I found I had very little stress. Or company.

All the inspections came up roses, and we closed the deal in late July.

I had already unpacked everything when I found out what the catch was: The place was haunted. Not by a ghost — I

could have dealt with a ghost — but with an aggressively living boy.

Baxter Browning loved to bark (what a title for a children's book!), but he didn't bark at Len. I went out to announce lunch, and there was Baxter, wrestling with a rumpled and smudgy four-year-old who was cackling laughter like a forty-pound hen.

"*Hello*," I said, loud enough to be heard over the love-feast on the lawn.

Dog and boy sat up and grinned at me.

"Hi," said the boy. "I'm thirsty."

"Are you?" I said. "Lunch, Baxter."

Baxter started for the porch. The boy stood up, tucked his t-shirt into his denim shorts, and came after him.

"Didn't your mother ever warn you not to go into strange houses?" I let Baxter in, but blocked the boy's way with my frowning body.

"I sure am hungry," he said. "And hot. And I need to Go."

"Why don't you? Tell your mamma you're hungry."

"I have to *Go*."

Did that stuff take the finish off treated lumber? I didn't want to learn the hard way.

"Come in," I sighed.

⌗ ⌗ ⌗

"My name's Len," he said, over a glass of milk and a paper napkin of *Crackin' Good* gingersnaps.

"Len What?" I asked. "And where do you live?" With a last name and a general address, I could probably track down his parents and give them a little unsolicited advice on child-rearing.

"Leonard Scott Marcus, 2342 Shepherds Pike, Shepherds, Indiana, 47112. 812-555-7384. My mamma's name is Shirley Lynn Marcus and my daddy's name is Leonard Paul Marcus. I got two brothers and three sisters. But I don't have a dog."

I got a pencil and pad and wrote down Len's vitals.

"You got a dog," said Len. "Do you have a little boy?"

I thought of all the boys of various ages I had declined to have over the years and said, "No, I do not have a little boy."

"Do you wish you had a little boy?"

"No, I do not."

That was the last either of us spoke until Len walked out of the house. "Thanks for the goodies. I'll come back tomorrow to play with your dog, since you don't have a little boy for him to play with."

And he was gone before I could tell him NO.

I called the number he had recited. A woman answered. I could hear Chaos shrieking in the background.

"This is Joy Crawford. I just moved in down the road from you. Did you know your little boy was at my house?"

"Which little boy? I have three — PIPE DOWN, I'M ON THE PHONE! — Oh, it must be Len. Just send him home, if he gets to be a nuisance. —YOU TWO. . . ." Click.

⧣ ⧣ ⧣

How do you tell a four-year-old you don't want him around, ever? "This is not a good time," I could manage. "It's time for you to go home now," I could manage. "I'll be busy tomorrow," I could manage. But, "Go away now and never come back. . ."? Couldn't be done.

In late August, Len started pre-school. Every evening I drove home to find a grubby urchin on my front porch with an armful of my dog and a stream of gossip about "the kids."

Darkness held no terror for him; the days grew short, but my headlights always picked out that figure waiting for me. I'd give him "goodies," listen to him while I got my supper started. Now and then he'd say, "Whatcha making? That looks good," but I had no trouble resisting the temptation. I'd just put everything on simmer and drive him home, then come back to my quiet and my solitude.

Len's parents, I discovered, were nice people. They cared for their children, but they had half-a-dozen; and Len, rather than being over-supervised, seemed to get overlooked. He made me come in once and look at his shelf (which is what you have when there are eight people and three bedrooms): It held a bird skull, a purple-quartz geode the size of a silver dollar, a magnetic travel-version chess set missing two pawns (one of each which, Len said, made it okay), and a dozen Little Golden Books. While I was there, one of his brothers gave him a Transformer; Len showed me how to change it from a lion into a man, made room for it on his shelf, and tucked it in his pocket.

#

My first Christmas Eve in the new house. We only worked half a day, and I looked forward to a Len-less afternoon. He was waiting for me when I pulled in.

"Did you have to work today? I been here all morning."

He had made me a present at pre-school: a bouquet of paper flowers, torn and crumpled and decorated with a unique patina of finger-grunge and *Elmer's Glue.*

So I didn't feel so stupid giving him the stuffed dog I'd ordered for him from an ad in the *New Yorker*.

#

I got back from Midnight Mass about 1:30, jumpy with that crystalline wakefulness that sometimes follows a victory over sleep. The sky was clear, the stars burned in quantities: more stars than I'd ever seen before. I let Baxter out of the house, and we walked.

As Carol, the former owner, had promised, the pool had frozen over. I had thrown a skating party for some of my closer acquaintances. Now, alone in the hours between Christmas Eve and Christmas morning, I had a fancy to see the sky reflected in the ice.

As we neared the pond, Baxter stopped, lowered his head, and whined.

"What is it, boy? Come on." I walked ahead, patting the side of my leg by way of encouragement.

Then I heard what Baxter must have heard: A weak, faded scream.

With one yelp, Baxter tucked his tail between his legs and scuttered for the porch.

I stood there, chilled inside my coat, and listened. Another scream, and another — pale and unreal, but undismissable.

"It . . . must be the ice breaking up," I said, and followed Baxter back to the house.

Sure enough, the next day there were cracks in the ice and the weather lady said a thaw had set in the night before.

# # #

The next year, the pond didn't freeze. I had a Winter Solstice party that included our all trooping out to the pond to throw feed pellets to the koi, each pellet to be accompanied by a wish.

I went out after Christmas Eve Mass with a packet of freeze-dried grubs. Baxter refused to leave the house. *Coward*, I thought.

But, as I neared the pool, I heard them: the screams. They seemed louder this year and I ran to the pool, convinced that, this time, they came from human lungs. In the water, two fat pink arms reached up; a round face, too small for the arms, between them . . . mottled . . . gaping. . . .

The panic passed, my vision cleared, and I saw the koi, lined up for feeding. I shook the grubs out in one grand spray and staggered home.

# # #

Len was in Kindergarten that year, and took upon himself the task of making sure I knew my letters, numbers, and colors. The next year, first grade: I heard about the girl he was going to marry, then the one he was *really* going to marry, then the one who was going to marry *him*.

The years passed, and every year brought a present: A cigar box pasted over with old Christmas cards (I supplied the cards). A brooch made of buttons (my buttons) stuck onto a flat wooden heart with a mass of craft cement. A dusty bottle of perfume with a yard sale sticker still on the bottom. A bird feeder made out of *Popsicle* sticks.

# # #

Winters were properly cold, and the pool was frozen over every Christmas Eve. I ventured just close enough to hear those muffled, icy screams; having heard them, I went back to the house with Baxter and cranked up Johnny Mathis.

I called Carol Pittinger, informing her that it was actionable to sell a haunted house without informing the buyer. She protested that the house wasn't haunted, just the pool, and only on Christmas

. . . my vision cleared and I saw the koi, lined up for feeding.

Eve, and only by a sound, and you couldn't call a sound a ghost, could you? She said the screams hadn't been there, so far as she knew, when she had bought the house. She first heard them two years after she moved in (and she named the year, as if I cared), and she had only heard them on Christmas Eve. She said she hadn't sold out because of "a little auricle illusion," as she called it, and one that only happened one night a year. . . .

"Yeah, yeah."

"Just don't go out there Christmas Eve. I didn't, the last year. Christmas is supposed to be nice and fun. . . ."

"Yeah, nice. Fun."

Not go out? Not listen? Not even check to see if the screams were there? Somebody was making those sounds — some PERSON was making them — or had, at some time past, maybe. I owed that screamer a listen, one human being to another.

⌗ ⌗ ⌗

That year, the weather turned freakishly warm around the solstice, and it was in the upper 60's on Christmas Eve. That year, Len didn't meet me with a present when I got home from work. He called to say he had a party (big 10 year-old — who needs a middle-aged grump, eh?) and that he would see me during the holidays.

The strange weather had me out-of-sorts and lazy. I usually took myself out for dinner and a movie before church, but this year I just boiled an egg and looked at the illustrations in a volume of Dickens.

A Christmas Carol, The Haunted Man, "The Trial for Murder" . . . So many of Dickens' Christmas stories had ghosts in them. Someone had told me once that ghost stories were a Christmas tradition in Victorian England. Bizarre tradition.

Then again, maybe not. Christmas *is* a sort of ghost story: The Baby is born with his death and resurrection already a done deal. I thought of a painting I'd seen of the Annunciation: Gabriel telling Mary about the coming Child while, on a beam of light, a tiny spirit descends carrying a cross.

Baxter and I sat alone by the gas fire while I tried to work up some enthusiasm for Mass, thinking I might not even go this year. My feelings were hardly celebratory.

Baxter jumped up with a yelp.

"What is it? Christmas present from a flea?"

Another yelp.

"It's started. Okay, let's listen. It's the least we can do, right?"

Baxter started to bark. He ran to the back door and scratched the panels, which is something he never does.

"You want out? But you never. . . ." I opened the door. He raced out and away, toward the pool. I was right behind him.

I could hear the screams louder this year than ever — less faded. . . . They were real!

The full moon cast shadows that picked out detail instead of obscuring it. As I ran, I could see the bank of the pool, with its rim of dead vegetation. In the tangle lay a "vase": a jar covered with adhesive tape and colored with shoe polish. I had made one, myself, when I was about ten. Some wilted carnations tumbled out of it had he stopped to get water for them? In too much of a hurry to walk around to the shelf, thought he'd just lean over, lost his balance, scrabbled for a hold and went in?

I only hesitated long enough to see Len come up — I wouldn't do him any good if I landed on top of him — and jumped in feet first.

Len was heavy in his sodden jacket, and he thrashed with terror. Holding him up, I went under. Baxter danced on the shore — scared of water, the worthless mutt. I kicked toward the shelving bank. I went under again, and got a lungful of water. Dumb kid. I started to see flashes of red. One more heft. One more. . . . Len left my arms as my foot slipped off the shelf. I pushed him toward shore and felt myself slide backwards. My chest was tight. I couldn't pull in enough air. I kicked feebly once again, slipped beneath the surface, and flickered into blackness. After the blackness came the light: light that shone through me, illuminating me inside and out. I heard familiar voices, but couldn't make out the words. I smelled roses, and fresh-baked bread . . . then it all faded back to black. . . .

#

I woke lying in the grass. Alive? I drew a deep breath. Alive.

Len sat next to me, water running from his jacket in rivers and from his eyes in streams. He was holding Baxter off me with one hand and clutching the vase of carnations in the other.

When he saw my eyes open, he let the dog go; I had to sit up to save myself from a spit-bath.

"Len . . .You pulled me out?"

"No, *you* got *me* out. You walked out by yourself."

"I did?"

"You went under. I couldn't reach you. I thought you were gone. . . ." Len's voice was still thin with fright. He shuddered and said, "Then your head lifted up and you opened your mouth and all this water p-poured out, but you wouldn't open your eyes. And you walked out as light as a feather, just so light . . . almost like you were floating. . . And you just sort of laid yourself down. But you wouldn't open your eyes, and I was scared. . . . I made this for you."

Ten-year-old Len held out his holy gift, and I took it with more gratitude than he would have understood.

Ten years ago, Len had been born. Ten years ago, screams had begun haunting the pool. Now, ten years later, I had followed those screams to the aid of my young friend.

He had given me his love, with no hope of return, and I had given him my life. And, in the true spirit of Christmas, both gifts had been blessed and reciprocated.

The pool is no longer haunted, on Christmas Eve or any other night, and the koi live there in peace.

The Christmas People

Jeannine Baumgartle

Sunday. A March wind swirled around the house. Eight-year-old Lila scurried through the morning darkness of the living room toward the kitchen with its square of gray illumination, half-tossing her present under the tree in passing. No one else was up yet, the thermostat was hers. She flicked it up before anyone could come out and tell her to take care not to waste fuel. There was never enough, of anything, food, heat, light, clothes, only presents — there were enough of those!

Pulling down the Cheerios from the shelf over the stove, she poured — some — into the bottom of her bowl, moistened them with milk and slurped into them. No spoon. You got more out of it this way, tongue and lips and teeth burying themselves up to the nose, sucking up the moisture around each crunchy little O.

Her bowl clinked as she put it in the sink, not quite covering the cardboard thud of a present dropped on the board floor.

"You didn't have to turn it up so high," her Mom complained, coming through the doorway. "Just enough to come on would have been fine."

"Sorry," Lila murmured, comfort dulling the authenticity of her answer.

She slipped around the corner to stand over the vent, the warm air ballooning her short nightgown, the envelope of heat like being hugged without being touched. God probably made furnaces.

"Your present's in there, Lila."

Mom knew she knew it was in there and only pointed out the obvious in grieved tones to make her feel bad. Luckily the furnace kicked off; the air coming out of the vent would get cooler and cooler. She could give that up.

Leaning over to pick up the box, she nudged one of the artificial branches, which flipped dust at her, sending her into a shiver of sneeze. Eeooo, she protested covertly, brushing at her gown and reaching more carefully this time. The ribbon on her present had been used so many times, most of the pre-formed loops were permanently mashed in. It tottered stupidly on the box from the all the layers of back-to-back tape.

She carefully pinched it free, and opened the faded corsage box. A new toothbrush. Orange.

"Thanks Mom."

A weary "You're welcome."

So. Lila tore off the cellophane wrapping, and traded the stiff-bristled new brush for old mush-face, which she had to admit needed replacing, even if it was like throwing away an old friend.

A sigh.

The kids at school envied her for being one of "The Christmas People." "Gosh, every day a present," Anna commented enviously, when she explained to her how it worked. Randy was so impressed he took the idea home to his folks, who told him it WASN'T a religion, it was a SECT. He came to school all bent out of shape, wondering what kind of awful things they did in that religion, and not until they got into a shouting match of accusations did the teacher intervene and make everybody understand that no sex was involved and that "sect" was like a branch off of a religion, kind of like a denomination, only — different, completely on its own.

She felt that difference in the way the other children regarded her, from the outside, as though they never expected to get in. "It isn't any big deal," she wanted to tell them, and flushed a little at the disloyalty of it, wanting to believe in her parents. Why they tried for it was beyond her. Rich people could give each other gifts every day if they wanted to, but for the three of them, (Dad was roped into the giving, though he seldom attended Meetings) it meant doing without, or making presents of things like toilet

A new toothbrush. Orange.

paper or baking soda. She gave an involuntary head-shake at the stupidity of it.

"Oh, thank you Lila," her mother's voice wafted through the house, pleased, and a little surprised. Lila straightened her shoulders. Mom liked the kleenex flower. At least she'd made it herself, and put time and effort into it. A little pink chalk in just the right places made it almost seem alive.

Tonight was meeting night. Meetings were at church, not a new one, but one they'd bought from the "First Christians" who'd outgrown it. Lila and her mom climbed the concrete steps and slipped inside the vestibule.

"Aggie!" her mom sang out, and her friend hurried over to embrace her. They chattered like birds, well-dressed birds, with purses and earrings and belts and heels. —Her mother could look nice when she wanted to. Lila stood there waiting for them, looking around, sort of, but not at anyone.

A minute or two later, Mother grasped her hand and they brushed past the ushers into the candlelit sanctuary and found a seat.

As always, Wisemen presenting their gifts to the baby Jesus were projected onto the wall. The altar was decorated with potted poinsettias and the organist played "We Three Kings." Sometimes the fall of the beat in the chorus wore a person down; that caravan was going nowhere. Same place every Sunday. Whoever invented the heavy-footed "Star of Wonder, Star of Night" was going in circles, looking down at the camels' feet instead of up in the sky.

The music stopped. "In the spirit of Christmas, we welcome all of you, sojourners to the manger of Christ. Let's take our song sheets, and stand and sing #2, Silent Night. The organist gave an introduction.

It was pretty, all the soft voices moving together, and then they were into the program: the announcements; the offering, the special music (if she heard one more screechy "O Holy Night" she thought she'd croak); the scripture, long ago memorized. You didn't hear it after a while, just let it roll over you like nursery rhymes before bedtime, halting phrases with unusual names and places in them like Quirinius, governor of Syria. And always Mary and Joseph and the babe, lying in the manger. Together. It was her own private joke, along with the "gold, Frankenstein and myrrh" she substituted for Jesus' gifts.

She wouldn't go up front for the children's sermon anymore. It was too humiliating to be head and shoulders above all the toddlers and kindergartners. They always played "Away in a Manger" during it, and she wondered if Jesus was embarrassed too, still in that manger as if he'd never grown up.

The sermon. The words went on and on. Still it was kind of nice sitting there in the dark, cuddled up against her mother's arm, yawning softly. The first part was always about how nice it was to be reminded every day that someone cared (she saw the orange toothbrush, in its holder on the rim of the rust-stained porcelain sink, and stared it into greenness behind her eyes, letting the drone of words carry her back to drowsiness) and ended with warning them to never let the Christ be killed.

It was over. They stood, and sang and took turns lighting their little paper-rimmed candles from the main one in front of the church, and filed out.

The car was cold. Lila's breath made fog on the windows. "Don't do that," her mother said before she could write in it with her finger.

Even though it was after her bedtime, they pulled into the Convenient store before heading out of town. Lila stuck close to her Mom as they rushed past the liquor display to the paper aisle.

"Your Grandma is coming over tomorrow night, and I don't have a thing for her," her mother explained in a harried voice, rooting through the gift-wrap for something half Christmasy. Anybody not in their immediate family had to have new wrapping paper and bows. Even the people at work. Even her teacher. —Whether Lila had money for the book-fair tomorrow or not. She despaired at the amount of junk they checked out with: jars of beauty cream; bagged candy her mother would make into decorative little arrangements to give to her co-workers; ink pens and mini-notebooks for Dad to give, and construction paper and paper doilies from which Lila would be expected to make her own gifts.

Tonight.

A Child-Like Christmas

Glenda Mills

If I could be seven again,
I'd lick candy canes until my tongue turned red.
I'd stop and stare at all the bright green and red lights,
Mesmerized by their twinkling.
I'd make a list of all I wanted,
A Barbie doll, a giant teddy bear, a black puppy,
With a red collar and floppy ears.
I'd sit on Santa's lap,
Maybe tug on his beard just to be sure.
I'd play Mary in the Church pageant,
Carrying my baby doll wrapped in a towel.
I'd eat Grandma's Christmas cookies,
Sing "Jingle Bells" loudly,
Over and over again,
Open all the Christmas cards,
Peek through the keyhole into "the room",
String popcorn,
And help decorate the tree,
In tinsel and lights and sparkling colored balls,
Like blotches of splattered paint,
Yellow, green, red, and blue.
On Christmas Eve,
I'd put the manger scene on Jesus' birthday cake,
And cut the first piece for Santa,
Leaving it on the mantle by the stockings,
With a big glass of milk beside the plate.
Then, I'd lay awake,
Listening for sleighbells and hooves,
Excited,
Lost in the joy and love that is Christmas.

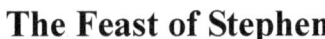

The Feast of Stephen
Ginny Fleming

At the front door, Dad impatiently tapped his foot. An hour before, Mom banished everyone from the kitchen. She busied herself packing contributions for the family Christmas dinner. It was Mom's fervent belief, Christmas wouldn't be Christmas at Grandma's house without a huge star-shaped sculpture of orange gelatin with bits of carrots suspended in time and pectin. Every Christmas, it quivered as if in fright in its place of honor on the huge harvest table's right hand corner.

Nobody but my bachelor Uncle Harold, ever touched the molded orange concoction. I'm not sure if he really liked orange gelatin or if Harold felt sorry for his older sister. But sibling love notwithstanding, I noticed Uncle Harold never failed to avoid Mom's Chili-Taco Surprise (the surprise was massive amounts of ketchup). Family love only goes so far. Even at Christmas time.

This year, we welcomed my other uncle's young wife into the family. Miyuki was a pretty girl who'd married Mom's youngest brother last year, while Uncle Stephen was stationed in Japan. We only knew her from letters and photos, having our curiosity peaked by transcontinental mail. What was she like? What were her customs? Would she know about Christmas? Family gossip had fair scorched the local telephone wires since we'd received word at Thanksgiving of Stephen and his bride's holiday arrival.

They were due in on the late afternoon bus from the big airport in Louisville. My Dad was chosen to give the young couple a ride to Grandma's house in his pickup; besides, all their luggage could be stored in the back of the rickety old Ford truck.

All week long I'd run around the house singing "When Stephen Comes Marching Home — Hurrah!" until my brother Jason cornered me outside my bedroom door and threatened the life of Chatty Cathy.

"If ya want the doll should keep talking," he snarled, "you'll shut your face. At least sing Christmas songs like you had a brain."

Dad loaded Mom's tasty holiday delights into the back of the truck, and the four of us squeezed into the cab for the cross-town drive to my Grandparent's huge cheery house.

I opened my mouth to begin a fresh chorus of "Stephen Comes Marching Home", squeezed uncomfortably beside Daddy and mashed under Jason's armpit. Jason leaned down and hissed: "Sing and C.C. gets it."

So, the ten minute trip across town was silent and decidedly unfestive, except for Mom wondering aloud about the safety of her Christmas delicacies stored not too snugly in the back. The strange smile on his face gave me the idea that Daddy didn't like Chili-Taco Surprise any more than Uncle Harold. I heard him mumble, "What I wouldn't give for a couple of good potholes." I believe Daddy hoped to lose the precious cargo out the tailgate of the rickety Ford.

We poured into Grandma's house like riotous holiday Gypsies bearing colorful wrapped presents. While Mom delivered her goodies to the kitchen, Daddy stashed the gifts under Grandma's six-foot tall aluminum tree (with accompanying electric four-color light wheel) before heading out the door to collect Uncle Stephen and his new bride.

All the cousins were there, and I quickly joined in on their reindeer games. Eddie, the cousin who most resembled Genghis Khan, had drug out the cushions from Grandma's parlor couch and created an impromptu gymnasium in the middle of the room.

Eddie's beleaguered little brother Danny held position as spotter. It was his onerous job to hunker-down at the end of the cushions and catch the tumblers should they stray off course and head for the folding stairs leading to the second floor (if our legs hit the stairs, not only were we disqualified, we caused an awful noise, which irritated Granddad).

We reached the climax of the game. Eddie and I were neck and neck (having already wasted Michael and Mildred, the two youngest cousins), and I was out for Eddie's blood.

I took my position at the head of the mat, ready to tumble for the gold, when all at once Granddad's angry voice filled the room. "What are you youngins doin' in here?" he boomed.

"Oh, no," I whispered to Eddie, "We made it all the way to Christmas Day — and now Santa Claus is going to turn that sleigh around." Eddie simply laughed. As I mentioned, Genghis was his role model. But, I was certain we'd killed that famed red-suited golden goose, and coal would be the lone gift in our stockings.

"Didn't Grandma tell you not to jump on her sofa cushions?" he growled.

I was near tears. Sure, we'd been naughty before, and been caught. But, not on the biggest day of the year. Was he going to punish us? Was Granddad going to snitch to the big guy?

Suddenly, the old man whooped and ran at the mat. Danny stepped back in alarm, certain Granddad was headed for him. With a cheery cry, the eighty year-old man turned a perfect double somersault, landing with his slippered feet crashing on the folding stairs. Amazing!

The booming crash brought Mom, Harold and Grandma from the kitchen. Granddad laughed uncontrollably, tears in his bespectacled eyes, flat on his back, his feet still on the second rung of the second floor stairs. The cousins pointed at Granddad and with one voice said: "He did it!"

"Crazy Old Fool," Grandma shook her head and returned to the kitchen. Dad burst through the front door with Stephen and a tiny black-haired woman in tow. She was dressed in a brightly colored robe (Miyuki later told me, the red and blue robe was a kimono).

Pandemonium ruled the next ten minutes, while our clannish family passed Stephen and his bride around from one kissing relative to the next. Poor girl.

From the midst of the melee, I picked up Miyuki's words. Bowing deeply, she said something like: *Ken itchy wa. Don't touchy mustache.*

"Okay," I wondered to myself, "Who's this Ken, why's his wa itchy, and who cares about his mustache?" Miyuki told me later, she'd said *Konichi wa . . . Doetashi Mashita*, which was simply part of a traditional Japanese greeting for her new family.

Led by Grandma, we retired to the kitchen, and formed a line at the buffet counter. Stephen and Miyuki were ushered to the head of the serving line. Being a gentleman, Uncle Stephen urged his bride to go first, and she shyly chose a plate. Taking delicate pieces of turkey, a small mound of mashed potatoes, and other choices of Grandma's holiday feast, she smiled at Stephen. Coming to the Chili-Taco Surprise, Miyuki frowned slightly, but took a cautious serving. Next, she spooned a dollop of carrot-filled orange gelatin over the ketchupy mixture.

We held our breath and looked to Uncle Stephen. Should we point out the social (and quite possibly gastric) mistake made by his Japanese bride? Or for the sake of Miyuki's feelings should we keep mum on the Chili-Taco Surprise/Carrot-Orange Jell-O faux pas?

"Sweetheart," Stephen said, realizing our dilemma, "I forgot to tell you about one of our family holiday traditions," he led her to the harvest table, "Newly married couples switch plates on their first Christmas together. You eat what I choose, and I eat what you choose." So saying, Stephen smiled and exchanged the plates. I watched his face as he dug into the gross-looking mixture placed between the mashed potatoes and turkey. After carefully chewing the opposing flavors, he smiled, turned to Miyuki, and kissed her cheek. In that moment, he became my hero, and I'll always remember that night as the Christmas we had the Feast of Stephen.

When it's Christmastime Down South

T.Lee Harris

Tiny lights winking amid swordlike fronds
Sinuously embrace tropical forms in a festive glow.
Great Grey-plumed Northern Snowbirds
(On the Southernmost leg of their migration)
Erect styrofoam snowmen and,
Thumb noses at the genuine article;
Ineffably pleased that,
Glimpses of white peeking through coarse blades of grass
Are sand rather than snow.
Cheerful manatee, poised on epoxy-resin tail,
Tightly clutching a gift-wrapped mailbox
(One hundred percent approved by the U.S. Postal Service)
Garbed in jaunty stocking cap and,
Awaiting his measure of greeting cards.
"Happy Holidays from Sunny Florida."

A Tree Out of Season

Joy Kirchgessner

"No don't cut it down," Kate implored. "Let's dig up a small tree and replant it after we've used it for Christmas."

"All right Kate," Jim said as he laid down the axe. "You're a hopeless romantic but I'll do as you like. I'll have to go back to the barn for a shovel. When I do replant the tree I'll put it right outside your bedroom window so that when you look out it will remind you of me when I'm gone off to war."

That conversation had taken place a week before their last Christmas, fifty years ago when they were just eighteen. Jim had never returned alive.

The two of them had grown up together where they had been neighbors. Jim had helped her parents on their farm up until the time he was drafted. If there was a field they hadn't crossed or a social event they hadn't attended, she couldn't remember it. Those were good days, bright ones filled with happiness. The two of them had such big plans.

Kate never married. She chose to live with her parents and upon their deaths, she, being an only child, inherited the farm. Though time, a bit of unavoidable neglect, and the weather had made its mark, the farm was classical — consisting of a white two-story frame house complete with gingerbread, a couple of utility sheds, a big red barn, a little woods in the back, and acres of rolling fields. She had long since rented those fields out to others for planting.

She had worked as a nurse at the local hospital before her retirement three years earlier. Now her days were spent either with dear friends or lovingly tending her yard full of hollyhocks and poppies and near her bedroom window, the Christmas tree.

The tree had never grown very large for some reason and these last few days the sap had been filtering through the bark of its branches as if it were bleeding.

"It was getting old, that's for sure," Kate thought to herself, "Probably leak a little around the branches myself. Whatever is happening to you old friend, doesn't look good."

Her concern for the tree had caused Kate to experience some unusual dreams where Jim would appear to her. It was like old times with picnics upon soft green grass under big shady trees or a night of light-footed dancing that lifted the spirit. In these visions she wasn't an elderly woman with aching bone and muscle, but one of eighteen — hand in hand with Jim. Jim, with his adoring eyes and beckoning smile. She would hate to awaken.

One afternoon as she pulled the weeds from her garden, she glanced up for a moment, casually catching sight of the tree. What she thought she saw made her do a double take. Was it moving or were her eyes and mind playing tricks on her? She walked over for a closer look.

The tree had been giving up the very essence of its life through its sugary sap; as a result, insects (hundreds of them), were harvesting it. They were so busy they didn't sense her presence. Bees, moths, butterflies of every description and color — no Christmas ornaments could match the mesmerizing flutter of all those wings.

That evening she pulled a comfortable chair up to her bedroom window so that she could look out and watch the movement on the tree as she nodded off to sleep.

Jim appeared to her again, more vivid than before. He stood before her with outstretched hand. She dazedly looked up from her chair, slowly reached out, and placed her hand in his.

When the first light of morning came, the insects had gone and so had Kate and Jim.

Visions of Sugarplums
Ginny Fleming

Baby rats. Baby rats. Gnawing at my gut, so tight. Baby rats . . . Baby rats . . . Nibble, nibble, nibble, bite. Oh, what fun it is to sing a junkie's song tonight.

This tuneless chant ran through Carter Fitzgerald Alexander's mind in opposition to the Christmas Music playing over the department store's sound system. The prerecorded festive carolers were scientifically test-marketed to soothe the subconscious of the bustling and frazzled holiday shoppers, increasing the profit margin by twenty-five percent and stuffing the stockings of the department store's stockholders. *Hark the Herald Angels sing; glory to the new-born King. . . .*

None of this savvy holiday business sales strategy meant jack-shit to Carter. And he cared even less. The vicious little baby rat named Withdrawal nibbled away at his concentration much as a flesh and blood rodent might dine fastidiously on a delicate Christmas cookie.

Alone on his break, he looked around the employee's lounge and groaned, wishing for a smoke; but the contract he'd signed denied smoking or drinking while dressed for the job. It wouldn't do for the little monsters to smell tobacco or liquor on their idol's breath.

He glanced at the wall clock. Time to return to his elaborate candy-cane decked throne. The plush red suit was hot, and the realistic-looking full white beard made his face itch. If he'd had the choice, he'd not be caught dead dressed in this fake-fur trimmed Santa suit. But, his needle-hunger dashed his choices against the wall.

"Who'd `a thought I'd be reduced to this crap job," Carter muttered, "Far fall from sailing on the Cape and blowing Daddy's money. Blowed Daddy's money all right. Stuffed it right up my nose. Seemed like I couldn't wait to move on to the liquid fire. Went from Pre-Med to needle-junkie in record time."

Carter bleated a ragged laugh, arranged his hated beard, settled the fancy stocking cap over his fake white curls and forced a halfhearted Ho-Ho-Ho through clenched teeth as grim practice. "Countdown to candy," he mumbled. "Two more hours and I'll have enough in my hand for two or three nickel bags. Merry Christmas to me!"

The smile on his face passed for Old St. Nick's merriment as the young man in the padded red suit returned to his post to listen to the little procrastinators. The tiny tots lisped their lists to the jolly fat man in the last few hours before the store closed on Christmas Eve.

Carter Fitzgerald Alexander despised every single wet-bottomed one of them, but his burning yearning gave him the necessary impetus to carry his act to the final curtain. The last two dimpled darlings bringing up the end of the line were decided Santa haters. Nothing Carter did moved these miniature mobsters. "Have you been good all year?" fell on deaf ears. "Ho-Ho-Ho" proved worthless. Shaking his silicone-padded stomach (like a bowl full of jelly) went unrewarded. "Tough room," Carter thought.

The high-school cheerleader hired as Head-Elf, roped off the candy-cane lined path leading to the "Big-Man", and Carter sighed with relief, checking his watch. Fifteen minutes, and he could head to the service desk and collect his check; he felt confident he could charm shy, plain Cindy Butz into cashing his holiday pay. Thirty minutes after that, he intended to make his pre- arranged meeting with T-Bone in the alley behind Floyd's bar. C.F. Alexander's festive plans included a truly *white* Christmas.

Despite his addiction-induced tremors, he found he nearly wanted to break into song as he waved and Ho-Ho-Ho'd his way to Cindy's desk. She didn't disappoint him. "Maybe the freakin' angels *are* smiling down on me tonight," he smiled to himself.

Tugging at the white beard, he thought for a moment about changing into his street clothes, bundled in his red velvet "Santa's Bag", but after checking his watch again, he headed for the store's back door still a dead ringer for the famous Fat-Man. Carter's white-gloved hand was on the door handle when he heard the little boy's voice coming from out of the darkness. Except for an inadequate light over the door, the alley was unlit. An unexpected blizzard had gifted the city with a three inch covering. Christmas would be white this year.

"Santa?" the soft, almost apologetic voice quivered in the blackness of the cold night.

Thinking fast, Carter shook his silicone-filled fat belly, and forced a laugh, his eyes searching the back alley for the hiding child. "Ho-Ho-Ho," he offered, "Santa's got to get to the city stable and hitch up the reindeer. You better run home now, and get to sleep so I can stop by your house. . . ."

"You never come to my house," the quiet little voice interrupted Carter's weak Santa Claus imitation. A small black child stepped from a snow bank into the anemic light.

"Surely. . . ." Carter stammered, "S-Surely I've visited you before. Tell ya what, Kid. When I get back to the North Pole, I'll check my books, see if there's been a mistake and. . . ."

The little boy raised his dark eyes up to him and the hollow words died on Carter's lips. "Never happened, Santa," the boy said matter-of-factly, "There's no mistake. Momma says you don't come to the Kitchens."

"Kitchens?" Carter shook his head, not following the child's meaning.

"Hell's Kitchen," he explained, as if realizing "Santa" was confused. Stepping closer to Carter, it was instantly apparent the little boy with skin as black as coal had missed too many meals.

He held his oversized corduroy coat closed with one hand, a broken zipper dangling like a price tag in the front, and Carter thought the boy's ragged jeans and wet scruffy shoes were obviously a gift from a larger relative.

He was clean; unusual for a child dressed in such rags.

God, Carter silently mused, *Kid's got pride in himself if he's got nothing else.* He shook his head, wondering at his own astute observation. *Why should I care about a scruffy little rugrat? Haven't I had enough of the greedy little wet-bottoms this month?*

"Tell me what I can do for you. . . ." Carter's words trailed off as he puzzled over why on Earth he'd offer his assistance. T-Bone was waiting with the much craved Christmas candy. It was cold, the source was jumpy and wouldn't wait in the alley long.

The little boy smiled. "My name's Tyrell. Come see Jaleka," he said, and his breath formed his quiet words in the cold air, "That's all I want. Jaleka needs you."

"Who's Jaleka?" Carter asked.

The little boy fell silent and turned to hurry out of the snow covered alley.

"Who's Jaleka?!?" Carter called after the ragged child.

The child's trailing words came from the south side of the alley. "Jaleka needs you."

The insistent little baby rat nipped at Carter's gut as if to remind him of his earlier promise. *Remember? You said you'd feed me!*

"Jaleka needs . . . needs . . . needs . . . ." the small boy's voice echoed back to him, and he cursed softly, prophetically knowing his meeting with T-Bone would be delayed.

"Tyrell?!? Who's Jaleka?!?" Carter screamed into the night and ran after the child, wishing for his Air-Jordans he now carried in the red bag wadded up in his clothes, instead of the thin thigh-length black leather boots that accessorized the plush suit. He saw the back of the running child as Tyrell ducked into

the next alley. "Wait up!" Carter yelled, "How'em I supposed find this Jaleka person if you don't wait for me!"

Five blocks later, having caught sight of the boy at each corner, he caught up with his ragged little tour guide. He grabbed Tyrell's slight shoulder and spun the boy around in front of a run-down brownstone. The boy looked up at the man dressed in the seasonal red workclothes and his dark brown eyes opened wide, "Jaleka," Tyrell said and pointed up at a window, "Jaleka. She needs you."

Winded and out of breath, "Santa" rested the plush red rucksack against his leg and followed the path of the child's pointing finger with his eyes. "Jaleka," Carter echoed the little boy's words, "Jaleka needs me. So? What are we waiting for? Take me to Jaleka."

Swallowed up in the oversized corduroy coat, Tyrell smiled. "Follow me," he said and pushed open the door to the ruined old house, "Fourth floor. She's waiting."

Carter followed the boy into the corridor and was hit almost immediately by the smell of hopelessness. The overpowering odor of urine and filth mingled in the air and clung to the dirty walls. The boy lowered his head and climbed the stairs, not looking back to see if Santa brought up the rear.

Topping the fourth floor landing, the child paused and waited for Carter to catch up. "She's in there. Wait, and I'll unlock the door," he reached inside his ripped sweatshirt and pulled out a key strung around his neck, "Momma says to always lock the door. I've got to watch after Jaleka. I'm older."

If you're older, Carter thought to himself, *then this Jaleka must be a baby.* He entered the dark apartment and automatically flicked the light switch. Nothing happened.

"Momma says we ain't gonna have 'tricity no more," Tyrell stated, deftly using a childproof lighter to light a candle stuck in a wine bottle. After he was satisfied the candle had caught, he carefully carried the small flame across the dingy room to an old fireplace. He folded back the metal fire shield, and turned toward Santa. "Momma says keep the fire covered when I'm not here. That's why I can't be gone too long — it gets too cold and Jaleka starts to cry," he bent down and threw a few scraps of broken furniture on the smoky fire, "I get the wood out of the trash."

"Where's Jaleka?" Carter asked, stomping his feet in the cold room. *How does this kid stand the cold?* Carter wondered, *I'll bet this room never gets anywhere near what I think of as warm.*

"Come on," said the boy. By the light of the lone candle he led Santa to a closed room and quietly pushed open the door. "Jaleka?" he called softly, "Jaleka, are you asleep? Look who came to see you. Aren't you a lucky little girl?"

"Tyrell? Tyrell? Is that you?"

She can't see through the darkness, thought Carter. "Ho-Ho-Ho!! Merry Christmas!" he boomed, announcing his presence to the child, "Ho-Ho—" the staged laughter died on his lips as the light of the candle reached the little girl's face. He could see she was probably two years younger than her brother, though they could have been twins for all he knew. Their skin tone was the same, their facial structure identical. The only discernible difference between sister and brother was Jaleka's unfortunate birth defect; congenital cataracts. "—Ho. . . ." the last *Ho* left his lips leaving him breathless.

"Santa Claus?!?" the little girl cried out. She sat up in bed and reached out her tiny dark hands towards his face, "Tyrell, you really really brought Santa Claus?"

"Don't be afraid," Tyrell took Carter's white-gloved hand and led him to the bed. Gently urging Santa to sit on the bed beside his sister, the boy placed Carter's hand into the searching hands of his sightless sibling. He whispered close to the Fat-Man's ear, "Don't be afraid. She just wants to feel your face. Jaleka needs to touch you. Jaleka needs you."

He looked into the face of the boy sitting beside him on the bed, nodded his head silently and leaned in to meet Jaleka's tiny grasping fingers. The little girl ran her hands reverently over Carter's rouged cheeks, gently felt around his eyes, and brushed her fingertips over his lips which still held a touch of red lipstick. Her mouth formed a perfect "O" as she lingered among the soft curls of Carter's beard.

"Ooooh, Santa," Jaleka breathed, "You look just like Tyrell said. He said you had a big beard, a red and white suit and kind eyes."

Kind eyes? Carter thought, *How would you know? I'm just a used up junkie . . . using children's dreams to get the money for my drugs.*

"Thank you, Santa," Jaleka said. A smile lit up her face.

"Yeah. Thank you, Santa," Tyrell echoed his little sister, "This is the best Christmas ever."

Carter looked from the little girl on the bed, still stroking his fake beard, back to Tyrell, beaming his happiness for his blind sister. "Come on," the man in the red suit snorted, "Aren't you going to ask me for something? A doll? A bike?"

Tyrell shook his head. "No," the little boy smiled, and for the first time Carter noticed the beauty in the child's face, "Why would we ask for things we don't need? Jaleka needed you — she needed to touch you and you came to the Kitchens. Momma says you should never ask for more than you need."

Carter stood up suddenly. "Where is this Momma you're always talking about?"

"Other room. She's sick." Tyrell helped his sister get comfortable in the bed, covering her with the thin quilt. He held his finger up to his mouth to quiet Santa.

"Sick?" Carter whispered. He felt the hair under his wig rise on the back of his head, and a shiver of premonition rushed up his spine, "What kind of sick? Headache?"

"No — Momma's been awful bad sick for a long time," Tyrell motioned for Carter to leave the room with him. The boy carried the candle, lighting the way for his red-suited friend. Stopping before the tiny apartment's other door, the boy looked up into

Carter's eyes, the candle casting light and shadows over the child's high cheekbones, "She hasn't left her room all week," he explained, turning the doorknob on his mother's bedroom door, "Be very quiet. Don't wake Momma."

Don't open the door! Carter wanted to scream, but the warning caught in his throat. Tyrell silently opened the door and the yellow candlelight fell over the bed.

"See?" the little boy whispered, "She's sleeping."

The flies were a dead giveaway.

Oh, my God! thought Carter, *she's at least two days gone. She's sleeping, and she's never going to wake up. . . .* He looked down at the small boy holding his finger to his lips ordering silence for his sleeping mother.

Carter licked his suddenly dry lips and gently placed his hand on his small friend's shoulder, pulling him from the bedroom. "Let your mother rest, Tyrell. She's very tired," he whispered, closing the door on a mother who'd faced many obstacles in her short young life and still given her children everything she could possibly give, to the cost of her own health.

Can't let them stay here, thought Carter, *Bad enough these kids don't have nothing on Christmas Day — but spending the holidays with a mother who's never gonna wake up — Man! Even a worthless junkie like me can't leave them here alone.*

"Let's go get Jaleka," Carter said as he ran his Santa-gloved hand over the little boy's head, "Let's get her into her coat."

"Jaleka don't got no coat."

Carter spoke around a sudden lump in his throat, "Okay. . . . We'll wrap her in the blanket."

Tyrell looked up at his jolly red-suited friend and took his hand. "Where we going Santa?" asked the little boy, trustful hope in his wide brown eyes.

"Damned if I know. . . ." Carter mumbled. He bundled up the sleepy little girl in her thin quilt.

✄ ✄ ✄

After exhausting the five other names on the other fourth floor apartment doors, and judging them unsuitable, Carter carried the little blind girl down to the third floor landing. The second door on the right declared the apartment to be the home of a Reverend and Mrs. Leroy Coleman. "Good people?" Carter asked Tyrell.

"Gives me candy sometimes," the little boy shrugged, "Momma says I can take candy from Reverend Leroy but nobody else. Momma says some people want to give kids bad candy. They're called strangers."

Yeah. Bad candy, thought Carter, *Tell me about it.* "Always listen to your Mo. . . . Always *remember* what your Momma told you, Tyrell. She loves you very much." He rapped on the door and wiped a tear from the corner of his eye, hoping the little boy wouldn't notice.

A short stout and balding black man answered the door and Carter's first thought was: *What the hell does this man have to smile about? Hell — I could be death knocking on the door.*

"Merry Christmas, Brother Santa!" Reverend Leroy boomed, grabbing Carter's free hand in a firm handshake, "What can I do for you on this glorious holy night?"

"Reverend. . . ." Carter began, hoping the words would come to his mind, "Reverend . . . I . . . ." he looked down at Tyrell, again grasping his gloved hand, "Reverend? Can the children come in and warm themselves?"

"Tyrell? Is that you?" Reverend Leroy crowed, reaching out and rubbing the child's head, "Hey, Connie! Company's callin'. Break out the milk and cookies." He took Jaleka from Carter's arms and handed the sleeping child to his wife. The smile stayed on his face until Connie Coleman hustled the two children into her kitchen. Carter caught the scent of fresh baked cookies as the door fanned closed behind the trio. "All right, now," Reverend Leroy lowered his voice, the cheerful tone gone, "What's really going on here, young man?"

"Listen, I don't have time for a lot of questions. Let's just say Santa visited two little kids and found I didn't have what they needed in my bag."

"Something wrong upstairs?" the reverend asked. His expression told Carter nothing would surprise this Man of God.

"Yeah . . . You could say that," Carter shook his head. He dug deep in his pocket and mumbled to himself, "Man, I can't believe I'm doing this. . . ."

"What, Santa?" the preacher asked.

Carter shoved the wad of bills into the black man's hand and turned, hurrying to the stairs, "See that the kids get warm clothes and shoes. . . .What am I saying? I'm sure you'll do what's right, Reverend," Carter started down the stairway and called over his shoulder, "Merry Christmas!" He laid his finger up side his nose and made his way down to the urine-scented corridor into the outside coldness.

The rosy-nosed reindeer making up the first of eight stamped its feet in the snow and snorted its hot breath into the frigid air. Carter Fitzgerald Alexander tugged halfheartedly at his long white beard, knowing in the last hour it had somehow magically transformed itself into real hair.

"Thanks for waiting for me, Fellas," he climbed up into the tiny black sleigh, snapped the reigns and crowed his exuberance to the heavens with a hearty Ho-Ho-Ho, his belly shaking like a bowl full of jelly.

Inside the dreary brownstone, a little boy knelt by the Coleman's cheerfully decorated windowsill and watched his hero take to the night sky, listening for the Fat-Man's famous farewell.

Finally feeling he truly fit in his clothes, Carter waved to the little boy and called out his blessing over the land: "Merry Christmas to all; and to all a good night!"

Christmas in July

Jeannine Baumgartle

It's only here
as far removed
from social obligation
as next year's Christmas
that my mind
will let down
carols, enter them
with the journalistic
detachment necessary
to read words,
discern what has been
done for me
in starlight
and angels
and the warmth
sudden and unexpected
of an infant in my lap.

Away in a Manger
T. .Lee Harris

The church organ thundered directly overhead, rhythmically bellowing songs of joy, celebrating peace and the birth of the baby Jesus. It wasn't a big, grand organ like the one in the plantation house back in Louisiana, but from Libby's place below it, it sounded like the voice of God itself. Close by in the darkness, she felt Papa shift to give Mama more room to cradle little Tad more snugly. He never cried if you held him tight, must be he felt safer that way. Libby wished she could feel safer; well that would come later with freedom.

Freedom. It had been whispering to them for a long time. Even her full name, Liberte, was her parents' native French for freedom — but that was a secret. It'd never do for the Masters to learn that tiny rebellion, so she'd been just plain old Libby for as long as she could remember. It was only in rare and private times when her own true name, and that of her brothers, Henri Jr, Louis and Teodore, were spoken. It was only then the secret hopes were breathed; the promise of the far north country of Canada and the glowing beacon of freedom. From the day Papa Henri and Mama Jolie had been sold by their old Master from Martinique, the island of their birth, to the cotton plantation in Louisiana, the tug of the now accessible Canadian forests had been growing.

Papa dreamed of disappearing into those great forests to live by hunting and trapping. It was lovely and thrillingly dangerous talk, but then the workday would begin again and they once more became Libby, Hank, Louey and Tad. Even Papa had lost his name, though not for the same reasons as herself. Papa Henri was a big man, bigger than anyone Libby had ever seen. Because of this, the new Master had predictably renamed him Goliath, and put him in the gold-braided uniform of a footman. The

Master of the sugarcane plantation had sold Henri and Jolie as a pair, and though that was a kindness, only Jolie had heard her own name used since that day as such a name was fitting to a lady's maid.

Learning the ways of the new Master and Missus had been slow, and Henri and Jolie bitterly missed their old home, but Libby's own arrival a few months later made the difference. Almost as soon as she could walk, Libby was being trained as a lady's maid, too. Though life was hard on the plantation, working in the big house had its share of benefits; like making journeys with the Master and Missus. Most trips had been simply to other plantations. The last had been to New Orleans.

Libby still recalled the city with wonder. In all her days, she had never seen its like: it seemed to stretch on forever, and was there any place on earth as full of beautiful people and places? Under the cover of concealing dark, her face crumpled as memory replayed how that dreamlike adventure had suddenly become a nightmare. Upon their return, they found that Hank and Louey had been sold and no amount of tears or pleading could persuade Master to tell them where they'd been sent. That had been last Christmas, now it was Christmas again and the ravaged remainder of their family huddled beneath the flooring of this Kentucky church.

Abruptly, the organ stopped. In the resulting silence she involuntarily glanced at the roof of their refuge. Imagination traced lighter lines where she envisioned the trapdoor under the pump organ to be. It was only imagination, though, for the little space had been carefully caulked all round so as to make it safer for those who hid there, and no light found its way in or out of the burrow. She grimaced. In spite of her scant sixteen years, her back was aching like it never had over the laundry kettle, and she wanted to straighten her legs like she'd never wanted before. That would come later, too. They were lucky for this hidden room, and if it was small, then so be it. They'd had cramped spaces before along the "railroad." According to what they'd been told, it was rare for a family to escape together and the accommodations had been designed for one or two persons, not four and especially not for one of such proportions as Papa Henri. Being below the floor of the church, the cubicle had at first been wretchedly cold, but after several hours with the four of them in such close quarters, it had become by degrees very warm — almost hot.

Feet shuffled above and presently the slightly muffled voice of the preacher began the sermon. Libby relaxed against the rough stone and wood of the closet and listened.

♯ ♯ ♯

She hadn't meant to fall asleep, but she must have, because a heart-stopping scrape brought her bolt upright as the organ rolled aside allowing light to seep around the hatch, invading their realm of darkness. As the boards swung back, the light was blocked by the young preacher's head and shoulders as he leaned down to whisper:

"You can come up now, it's almost time to move out. I have food and drink, it's naught but bread and cheese, but the coffee's fresh and there's a bit of milk for the little one."

Libby was the last out, and she blinked as her father's powerful hands lifted her out of darkness into the unaccustomed brightness of the lamplit church. Accepting her share of the humble meal gratefully, she stole a shy peek at the preacher, who asked to be called Brother Victor. She'd never seen a man quite as white as this one; not only did he have the palest eyes, but his hair was so light so as to have almost no color at all. Now, with the lamp at his back, his colorless hair transformed into a glowing circle of gold around his head. The holy folk in the colored glass windows of the big New Orleans church she'd seen had glows just like that.

Henri and Victor pushed the organ back into its place and chocked the wheels while Jolie divided the food laid out on the front pew. Inspecting the floor for telltale markings, the young man asked:

"Are you folks all right? Wasn't too cold for you down there?"

Jolie laughed a little and answered:

"Oui, Monsieur Victor, it was fine, it got quite warm after a bit, but we'll take that over the cold any day. We aren't any of us used to it."

The young man smiled and nodded, saying:

"I'd imagine not, being from so far south and all." Pleasantries tended to, his face clouded:

"There were two strangers in the congregation tonight, rough-looking men. They claimed to be farmers, and they probably were — once. But I'll lay it's been many a year since their hands touched a plow."

Henri looked up from his bread and worked to swallow with a throat suddenly dry:

"Slave-catchers?"

"Looks like, though I can't be certain." Victor fell silent, then added:

"Look, if you'd like to stay here for a few days, you're more than welcome to. I can easily get a message to the next . . . ."

Henri shook his head with finality:

"Mais non, we come too far to stop now. Long's they got no dogs, we keep on."

The preacher eyed the solemn group skeptically, but said only:

"You've also come too far to be taken." Abruptly he stood and striding for the small back door, announced:

"We better be getting the wagon ready, then."

Libby tucked her remaining food into the small bundle that held Tad's and her belongings, and clutching it, followed quickly.

⧲ ⧲ ⧲

She leaned against the barn listening to the muted sounds of the horses and jingle of harness. It was cold outside, but that made little difference in the pleasure of fresh air after the long day's confinement. Pulling the light shawl around her shoulders, she frowned into the cloudy sky above. A step crunched the frosty yard beside her. Stifling a gasp she pivoted as gentle hands draped a blanket around her quivering shoulders. Brother Victor's familiar voice broke the crisp silence:

"It's awful cold out here tonight, I thought this might be welcome."

Smiling in the filtered moonlight, she settled the blanket around her and answered softly:

"Thank you, it is a mite nippy."

"You maybe should come inside, it's not that much warmer in there, but it'll keep the wind off you. Can't say I like the look of those clouds, neither, looks like they might be thinking about dropping snow soon. That could make trouble for us."

"I'm not so worried about the snow as I am about that North star been leading the way up here. Those clouds keep scooting betwixt him and me. Just like now! And it gives me a nasty turn every time." Catching his amused glitter, she grinned ruefully and admitted:

"Oh, I know it's plain superstitious foolery, and Papa's al'us saying 'the darker the night, the better for us,' but somehow I feel better when I can see that star. Puts me in mind of the wise men you talked about tonight."

Returning his gaze to the overcast skies, he remarked:

"I was thinking about just that when I wrote that sermon. It is my fervent prayer that like the Magi, you folks'll find what you're looking for under the star's light, too. But look at you, you're still shivering, we better get you inside before you freeze solid."

Taking her by the elbow, he began to guide her toward the inviting rectangle of light spilling across the barnyard from the lantern inside, adding with a grin:

"I also don't feel right about leaving all the work to your Pa, but, truth to tell, I was commencing to feel a novice there. Your Pa can sure handle animals. I've never been able to get that old bay cuss to . . . ." Breaking off abruptly, he froze in mid-stride and stared at a darker patch at the edge of the neighboring thicket, his fingers tightening uncomfortably on her arm. Suddenly he gave her a shove toward the door, hissing urgently:

"Run! Tell your Pa we got visitors."

Not daring to look behind her, she loosed her grip on the fluttering blanket and ran for all she was worth. Over the frantic pounding of her heart, she heard swearing and heavy footfalls crossing the yard, then a shout. Glancing back as she entered the warm scents of horses and hay, she saw two large silhouettes overtake and fell the smaller form of the preacher. Voiceless with terror, she entered a scene that told her a warning was unnecessary, as she saw her father hurrying her mother and brother up the stairs into the hayloft. Suddenly, the choking silence of their fear was broken by the sharp click of a rifle being cocked outside. They froze in place as a gruff voice rang out:

"Hi! Hold off, you half-wit. A shot'll bring the whole town down on our heads. We's too far north for that kind of truck."

A lighter voice slurred with drink whined:

"But what we gonna do with 'im, Evans? He done seen us."

Although they hadn't heard the man called Evans moving, the nearness of his voice as he replied spurred them back to life:

"Jes' haul him in here. They's quieter ways to finish a fellow and we got us some runaways to catch."

Before she knew what was happening, her grim-faced father had swung her into the manger and covered her completely with the sweet-smelling hay. As she lay back, a hard object struck her sharply on the face. Stifling a cry, she clawed at the object nearly sobbing her relief at discovering it to be only an old pitch fork buried in the hay with her.

Turning her head, she found she had a narrow window on the outside world through a gap in the hay. Standing close enough to touch, was Papa, legs set and clutching a chunk of wood in one hand. Moving like an enraged bull, a red faced white man entered her field of vision, and ducking under the rude club, bore her father to the hard-packed ground where they struggled for possession of the weapon.

Long years of manhandling baggage had given Henri the edge and momentarily, he arose astride his foe. As he drew back a massive fist to deliver the final blow, a thump like the splitting of an overripe melon sounded. Even though the enraged slave went slack-jawed on the first blow, the man who'd struck from behind, struck again, and his sand-filled sap burst with the force spraying its gritty contents over the combatants.

While the second pulled chains and irons from a sack, the first pulled himself from under his unconscious opponent, spat sand and snapped:

"You sure took your time!"

Nodding toward a motionless form half in the door way, he said:

"Well, you told me to tote that one in here, Evans. He ain't exactly no sack of flour, is he? Nor is this one! Wheew! This one'll bring in a fine piece of money one way or t'other."

Evans pulled his chin thoughtfully:

"Surely will. Now, this 'yer buck looks to fit one of them items from the handbill we seen yestidy." He spat more sand and wiped his mouth with the back of his hand musing:

"'Pears to me they was more than one in that bill, too. Well, we seen the darky wench this white trash was jawin' with run in here, and they ain't no way out the back. Find where she's hidin' and drag her out . . . ."

"But what about t'other fella? Thought you said we'd do him in here."

"*Dammit, Coleman!* Would you get that out of your head? You'll get your way in due time, now make yourself useful and get up in that loft!"

At his words, wisps of hay sifted down between the floorboards propelled by some unseen movement. At the sight, Evans' face contorted in a leer of calculation:

"Well, well. Looks like the mice is kickin' up." Kneeling beside the fettered slave, he pulled a sharply gleaming knife from his belt and pressed its point against Henri's temple. Blood welled where the point met flesh and trickled down the blade's shiny surface. Evans lifted his face to the loft and called:

"You there in the loft, come on down now, less'n you wants to see the big buck here sliced up some. Won't make no never mind to me, he'll sell as well with a scarred-up face as without."

Aroused by pain, Henri's eyelids fluttered and sprang wide with anguish as he saw his wife stand and step toward the ladder. As she descended, the young man emitted a low whistle, exclaiming:

"Looky what we got here — pretty little bonus to keep us warm on this cold night."

"*No!!*"

With his outraged bellow hanging in the air, Henri started out of Evans' grasp and lunged for the younger man. Head still reeling from the blows, his legs entangled by the heavy chains, he fell heavily to one knee far short of his target. Laughing, Coleman raised his rifle and swatted the shackled man to the floor with the barrel, but the younger man's grin evaporated as Evans leapt forward with an oath and buried the knife to its hilt in his ribs. Coleman dropped without another sound.

Evans stood, and wiping the blade on the dead man's shirt, muttered:

"Damned fool's been nothing but trouble since we struck out. Good riddance to bad rubbish, I al'us say." Backing up against the manger to keep everyone in view, he brandished the knife, commanding:

"Jus' cause they's one less down here, don't make nothin' no different. C'mon down 'fore I come up there after you."

To Henri's amazement, the slave catcher's thick neck sprouted a line of black holes. Evans' eyes widened in surprise and his mouth opened, but all that emerged from the gaping lips was a spill of bright crimson that oozed down his chin and spattered across the dirty shirtfront. With the same abruptness, his knees buckled, and he tumbled to the packed earth. Just behind the crumpled body, Libby knelt in the manger, flecked with wisps of straw, and transfixed by the twitching object before her. The old pitchfork clenched in her white-knuckled hands glistened red in the dancing illumination of the lantern.

⋕ ⋕ ⋕

A safe distance from town, they paused for Papa Henri and Brother Victor to roll the bodies into a wooded ravine. It was none too soon for Libby, and she shuddered afresh at the tumbling, crashing they made until they struck whatever passed for bottom. The long-threatened snow began to fall as Victor voiced his hasty request that the Almighty have mercy on the two souls so abruptly delivered to His care that night. Then the wagon lurched forward resuming its northward journey.

With one final glance at the darkness that swallowed the corpses of their enemies, Libby watched the big wet flakes of sparkling white settle in a concealing blanket. Wrenching her eyes from the remembered horror, she moved closer to her mother and baby brother in their shared blanket, and turned her gaze back onto the beckoning star.

The Touch of a Child
Glenda Mills

Melchoir could not understand the quietness in the marketplace. It wasn't that he missed the loud voices bickering over a shekel more or less. Still, he was a curious man. He thought for a moment, trying to remember what little he could about these Jews and their ways. It was not yet the Sabbath, so why were the vendor's stands vacant? As he looked around the empty market, he saw a throng gathered just outside the city gate. On the far side of the crowd, three crosses were silhouetted against the sunlight of an early afternoon sky. He had heard of Roman crucifixion, a barbaric practice if you asked him, but he'd never actually seen one. His curiosity grew, drawing him away from the vacant market to the hill where the people were watching others die.

The multitude was so large that Melchoir dismounted his camel, leaving it with his servant, and pushed his way through the crowd until he reached the front. There were three men hanging suspended by their outstretched arms, gasping through grimaced faces for a small breath of air, then collapsing in exhaustion from the effort, only to repeat the ghastly ritual moments later.

The two men on either side seemed ordinary enough, common thieves being executed for their crimes. The man in the middle, however, the man who held the crowd's attention almost exclusively, was no ordinary man. Even the inscription above his head bore his crime as "King of the Jews". Melchoir tried to look upon his face, but it was bloody and swollen. His beard had been pulled out in large clumps, his hair was matted to his brow with blood, and his eyes and mouth were almost swollen shut. Melchoir quickly looked away. That's when he noticed the woman.

She was standing at the base of the middle cross, clinging to it, crying uncontrollably. She raised her head to gaze upward. Even through the tears, Melchoir recognized her.

"My stars," he said in a hushed whisper. "My blessed, blessed stars, it's her. It's the Child's mother."

Melchoir hadn't seen her for over thirty years. The lines on her tanned face and the callouses on her hands could not mask the beauty that emanated from her. He stared at her in all her sorrow and let the image of her face take him back to the first time he'd seen it, radiant and smiling.

It had been curiosity that had driven him to make the long trip thirty years ago. A star had appeared, a star that was brighter and larger than any star he'd ever seen. Astrology was his craft, so he knew this star meant something — something special. He just wasn't sure what. From its size, all indications were that someone of royalty or great importance was involved. The brightness stood for a beginning — a birth, a coronation, something like that. He mapped the star's location and discovered that it was stationary, resting over a geographical site known as Judah, a small Jewish province under Roman control. He searched his archives and came across some ancient prophecy about a Jewish king who would be born. He hated the Roman Empire and decided that he wanted to meet this man who was destined to overthrow the tyranny of Rome and lead his people to freedom. He sent messengers to two fellow astrologers, Balthasar and Gaspar, who lived in nearby lands. They had also seen the star and quickly accepted his invitation to travel with him to meet this king.

The journey took over a year. They did most of their traveling at night when the star could be seen. During the days, they hid from the heat as much as possible, sleeping in the early morning and late evening. The few towns they passed through gave them a chance to enjoy fresh food and water, as well as get needed supplies. There were a number of times Melchoir wondered what they would find at the end of their journey. He hoped he hadn't convinced his friends to invest their time and money on some useless search, a dream based solely on a large, bright star and an ancient prophecy from some foreign civilization. He wondered if the heat of the desert had impaired his logic.

When at last they came to Jerusalem, they began to ask the people there where the Jewish king was. They were answered with blank stares and loud oaths of allegiance to Caesar. After three days of inquiries, they had come up with nothing. Granted, a man who was planning a revolt against the Roman government would need to keep a low profile, but this was ridiculous. Melchoir heard that same voice of self-doubt grate in his ears, intensifying his anxiety with each passing day.

On the morning of the fourth day, six Roman soldiers came riding into the astrologers' camp. One soldier dismounted, asking loudly to see the men who had been inquiring throughout the city about some Jew who thought himself a king. Melchoir left his tent in great haste, driven by dread not only for his own safety and that of his group, but also for this man that he had yet to even meet. Balthasar and Gaspar soon joined him, standing in fear before the armored horsemen with their glistening shields and spears.

"We come by decree of King Herod. He has heard of your search for a man of royalty and wishes to discuss the matter with you at his palace. The three of you will come with us now."

Of course, they had done just as the soldier said. What other choice did they have, given the circumstances? When they arrived at the palace, they were led to the throne room.

"Kings are so predictable," Melchoir thought to himself, eyeing the marble, gold, jewels, and intricate tapestries.

The man on the throne was short and stocky with thick dark hair and a dark beard and moustache. His face showed no signs of exposure to the oppressive heat and blistering sun outside the palace walls.

The guard who had spoken at the camp stood before the throne, announced them, and moved aside, motioning them forward.

"Welcome to my humble dwelling. I understand you have traveled a great distance in search of a Jewish king. Is this true?"

Melchoir felt obliged to answer himself, since this had all been his idea in the first place.

"My Lord," Melchoir began, bowing as he spoke, "We are astrologers, gazers of the stars. Last year, we saw a star, a large bright star. We believe this star tells of a man of royalty or great importance who has just started his reign either by birth or coronation. We have come, drawn by the star, to see the man whose kingship is proclaimed by the heavens."

"I see." Herod paused for a moment, stroking his beard. "Might I inquire further as to why you believe this king is in Jerusalem?"

Melchoir did not like the idea of relinquishing any more information than necessary, but he knew of the Roman's reputation and decided he would have to cooperate of face dire consequences, not only for himself but for Balthasar and Gaspar as well.

"I calculated the star to be at rest over this province. Ancient Jewish prophecies speak of a king, a descendant of the line of King David. That is why we have come here to search."

There was a long silence. The troubled look on Herod's face began to soften and relax. By the time he spoke again, there was a slight curve in his lips that could well have been a smile, although it was hard to tell through his beard.

"I, too, have heard of this Jewish prophecy. You see, I am Idumean and, therefore, a half-Jew. I do not know where this king is to be found. I believe you will find that you seek a child. My contacts are vast and thorough. I would know if there was a man asserting kingship of any kind. However, a child's destiny would be something else altogether. When you find this child, come back and tell me where he is so I may visit him as well. As I said, I am a half-Jew myself and would very much like to meet the child who is to fulfill such an important prophecy. Go now, and good fortune be with you in your search."

With that, Herod got up to leave the room and the astrologers were escorted out of the palace. Melchoir felt uneasy over the meeting with Herod, but there wasn't time to reflect on why. They weren't any closer to finding this prophetic child. After sleeping some in the afternoon, they waited for nightfall, hoping the star itself would guide them on.

When the desert sky again grew dark, the star appeared, brighter than ever. It's position was slightly different than it had been the previous nights. Melchoir began mapping and calculating. The star had moved southward. The closest town to the south of Jerusalem was a place known as Bethlehem some five miles away. They decided to continue their search there.

All through the night, the caravan traveled, reaching the edge of town just before daybreak. After sleeping for awhile, they entered Bethlehem, stopping at every inn and shop, inquiring about the birth of a king. No one seemed to understand their question, nevertheless have any idea where the child was. At last, the three weary men came to an inn at the edge of town, a run down, simple place with a cave behind it that smelled as if it were used for a stable. They went in to have a drink of water and perhaps a bit of bread and mutton.

When the owner greeted them at the door, Melchoir asked him about the child king. At first, he said that he knew of no such child. Then he grew silent for a moment.

"Wait, wait. I do remember. Back a year or so ago, when Quirinius ordered the last census, there was a young couple. They came to my door looking for lodging. There were no rooms anywhere in town, and I was their last hope. I had no rooms either, but I couldn't bear to turn them away, what with the woman being so heavy with child. I offered them the stable, it was all I had, and they eagerly accepted. Later that night, I heard a baby crying. I was glad then that I had not sent them away."

"Could this child have been the king we seek?" Melchoir asked, hoping he had at last found part of the answers to his questions.

"A king," the man said with a smirk. "I don't see how a king could come from such poverty. These people had nothing. Still, there were the rumors about the shepherds."

"Shepherds?" Melchoir pressed the man to continue.

"Yes. Shortly after I heard the baby crying, I fell asleep. It had been a very busy day, so I slept soundly. The next morning, when I went to the marketplace, there was talk that a group of local shepherds had seen some heavenly vision and had come to my stable to see the baby. I didn't put much store in it all at the time. Sitting out in a field alone for hours on end can make a man see and hear lots of things, you know what I mean. Anyway, if you're really curious, the couple lives here in town. The father owns a carpentry shop that he runs from his home. That's all I can tell you."

The travelers thanked the innkeeper and set out once again, encouraged by what they had learned.

It was nightfall before Melchoir and his companions found the carpenter's house. As they stood outside the simple home illuminated by the light of the large bright star which was resting directly above the dwelling, Melchoir knew that the gold he had brought as a gift would be greatly appreciated. He had devoted his life to studying the stars, and, for the first time, he wondered what this all could possibly mean. There was no doubt that this was the place the star had chosen as their destination, but why? Hesitantly, he knocked on the door.

A man with bare feet dressed in a handmade robe opened the door. His hair fell in dark wavy locks across his shoulders and down his back. His beard, though not groomed, was neat and clean. The callouses and wounds on his hands and the weariness in his eyes marked him as a laborer. The sight of a wealthy caravan outside his home caused the man to pull away from the door slightly. Before he could recover from his surprise, Melchoir spoke.

"Please forgive our intrusion this night. We mean you no harm, I assure you. We are astrologers who have followed a star which first appeared in the heavens over a year ago. It has come to rest directly above your home. We believe that here is where we will find the prophetic king we seek. We bring gifts for him and desire to present them personally so we may pay homage to his royalty as well."

The man listened quietly to all that was said. Then a gentle smile formed on his wind-chapped lips.

"All visitors are welcome here. My name is Joseph. My wife, Mary, and our Son, Jesus, the Child you seek, are inside. Please come in."

Melchoir, Gaspar, and Balthasar, gifts in hand, entered the small home. A single oil lamp sitting in the center of the room on a crude wooden table provided the only light. A young woman sat at the table, sewing a small shirt. She looked up when the men walked inside.

"Mary, these men have come a very far distance in order to see Jesus. God led them by a star from their home to ours. I have told them they are welcome here."

The woman rose in silence and walked over to where her husband was standing. Melchoir had seen countless women in his days laden in gold and jewels, wearing gowns from the finest silks, but never had he seen a woman as beautiful as her. She wore simple clothes of rough hand spun threads. Her hair was long and straight, as black as a desert night. She did not have any jewels around her neck or gold on her wrists. He wondered for a moment what it was that made her so captivating. Then his eyes met hers, and for the first time, he understood. It went beyond the gentleness and love that was there to a place somewhere deeper, where he found a sacredness stronger than any he'd ever seen in another person, even the holy men of his land. He stood in awe before her, drinking in her sacred nature through those piercing brown eyes.

"Mama!" The Child's voice rang out across the room, jarring Melchoir from his thoughts.

The Child came running, arms outstretched, laughing. He grabbed his mother just below her knees and hugged her. He wore a nightshirt made of the same rough material as his parents' garments. His curly brown hair bounced as he ran. Even in the midst of such normalcy, Melchoir felt that same holiness he had sensed in Mary, only the feeling was amplified ten-fold. He was so overwhelmed by the Child's presence that he fell to his knees in worship. He kept his eyes to the floor, unable to look upon such a sacred person, feeling suddenly unworthy to be in this humble room despite his wealth and power. Every unkind thing he'd ever done came back to haunt him, and he lowered his head even more.

Lost in thought, Melchoir did not notice the Child standing beside him at first. Gradually, he became aware of Jesus' warm breath on his cheek and saw his tiny bare feet on the floor beside him. He gathered his courage and slowly raised his eyes to look upon the Child's face, which was round and glowing, tanned from playing outdoors, with dark eyes that twinkled like the stars Melchoir knew so well. Before he could do or say anything, the Child threw his arms around Melchoir's neck as if he'd known him all his young life, and hugged him.

"I love you," the Child said sweetly, then turned and toddled back to his parents.

Three little words and a simple touch from a child, and yet the feeling of peace that he knew at that moment had stayed with him over all these years. He did not understand all that had happened that night, but he had discovered more holiness and love in that one-room home than in all the elaborate temples and luxurious palaces he had visited before or since.

Melchoir and his companions spent the night with the holy family. All three of them had dreams during the night warning them not to return to Herod, so the next morning they set out for home, taking a different route that kept them away from Jerusalem.

Melchoir had thought of the Child and his parents often over the past thirty years, wondering what became of the boy who was destined by the stars to be King of the Jews.

King of the Jews. The phrase echoed loudly in his mind, sending a wave of horror sweeping over him. For the first time, he forced himself to actually look closely at the man in the middle, allowing their eyes to meet. The love, the holiness were still there, somehow stronger and more intense than they had been before. The man cried out and then slumped forward for the last time. An unexpected wave of despair drove Melchoir to his knees, heavy sobs shaking his body. What he had experienced in the dim light of that small house had felt so real. Kneeling in the cold shadow of the cross, he wondered how he could have been so wrong.

Melchior tried to look upon his face. . . .

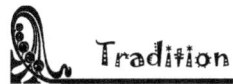

Tradition
(with apologies to Ogden Nash)
Marian Allen

I've never been able "to see
if reindeer really know how to fly," but I know a Christmas tree
sure can.
All you have to do is take a man—
my husband, for example—
take him to the woods and let him trample
around in the snow, looking for the very best
tree he can find. Let the rest
of the family stay home where it's warm, or let them come
and argue and call one another's choices "dumb."
Choose a tree that looks just the right
size for the room. I guarantee you that the height
of that tree will be at least two feet over,
a fact which you must let your man discover
before he takes the tree inside
so, while everybody else goes in for popcorn and hot chocolate,
    he can stay out on the porch and cut lengths off the trunk
    until the tree is less high than it is wide.
Then
let him in.
Next, your man must spend an hour looking in the basement for a
    tree stand and then you must find it in a minute in the
    attic.
Your man's language will become emphatic.
Finally, let the tree not fit the stand, and let it lean once
    it's whittled down to size, and let it fall over unless
    somebody's holding it, and let everybody start fighting over
    what ornaments to use and how much tinsel, and let them all

get mad and go to separate rooms declaring that they don't care if the tree never gets decorated and, when all this has been done, open the back door and stand by.

That tree will fly.

Bethlehem
Dirk Griffin

One
birth—
ancient—
rings across
generations past:
altered in form, spirit never
lost, though it divides
nations; joins
lost souls
in
love

(Not-So) Happy New Year!
Joanna Foreman

My twelve-year-old son didn't hear it — black vinyl buds streamed the racket he called music into his ears, blocking out reality. But my husband and I, already on edge, were startled when the phone rang.

"The police are on their way up," the lady at the front desk informed me.

I surveyed the motel room, blankets and sheets sprawled on the floor, very few personal belongings, and my first thought was that we would most definitely be blamed for the damaged bottom dresser drawer. My husband had kicked it with a vengeance when he realized we'd been robbed during the night. Cheap, pressed wood, the cracked drawer-front had dropped with a clunk to the floor.

We'd slept right through the burglary, as difficult as that was for me to believe. Our first clue that something had gone wrong was when my husband got up and went to pull on his jeans.

"Where did you put my pants?"

I sighed. (Why do men think women know where everything is at all times?) I wanted to say that his pants would be right where he'd dropped them, but I would've been wrong. They were later found on the ground on the other side of the motel, sans hand-tooled leather belt and wallet.

My response to his pants question had been that I didn't do anything with them. His next question, "Did you open this door?" finally woke me up enough to sit up in bed.

"What door are you talking about?" He was standing at the outside wall which was entirely covered top to bottom with drapes.

"This one," he said as he pulled back the curtains. I hadn't even been aware that our cut-rate room had a sliding patio door.

♯ ♯ ♯

It was the night before New Year's Eve, and we'd hugged and kissed every last family member in Houston around noon, promising to return next Christmas. He'd driven all the way to Jackson, Mississippi when I caught him nodding off twice. I wanted to stop but he claimed he could make it just fine. Then, he nodded off the third time. I demanded that he find a motel — and pronto! He put a frown on his face that I could plainly see in the darkened car, jerked the vehicle off the road at the next exit and stopped abruptly in front of the lobby of the first motel he saw.

"There," he said. "Is this what you want? This dump?"

"I don't care about the scruffy appearance of the place, I only want a bed!"

We carried some of our luggage into the room and crashed. We'd finish our holiday tomorrow, refreshed, with a final eight hour drive.

♯ ♯ ♯

I felt a cool breeze when he pulled back the curtains; the patio door was open slightly. I looked around the room and realized that everything I'd brought in was gone. My purse and backpack had been made in Mexico of hand-tooled leather and purchased in Texas. "They've taken everything," I exclaimed. "How did they do that without waking us?"

The word violated floated heavily in the air. That's when he kicked the dresser drawer.

I said, "Well, now — that's gonna help a lot!"

"It helps me," he said. I was impressed; I'd never seen him that angry.

My son barely opened his eyes. He grappled under his covers to make sure his Walkman was intact. He'd slept in his clothes and hadn't lost a thing. He rolled over and went back to sleep.

Two officers came into our room. They questioned us and
said there was an aerosol spray on the black market that is used
to keep people from awakening. I didn't believe them, because
if that were the case, wouldn't the criminals have to don gas
masks? I mean, it's not like this place was the Ritz! The cops
said they'd been called to this same motel at 11:00 the
night before because guests had seen three young men piling
chairs up and climbing them to second-story rooms. The
officers' appearance had scared the would-be perpetrators away
and they hadn't been expected to return. We'd checked in just
before midnight.

The motel manager was sympathetic at first, and kind
enough to drive me to a local grocery where I retrieved a check
American Express had wired to get us through the day.

I inquired of her upon our return, "Does the motel carry
liability insurance for this type of thing?"

"No," she snapped. "It is our guests' responsibility to
securely fasten their door locks before retiring."

"Oh. Really? Well, I would've appreciated it if you'd alerted
us to the fact that we actually had a patio door when we checked
in. With those heavy drapes covering the entire wall, and
the darkness outside, there was no evidence of it. Especially
considering the police were called here one hour before we
checked in. They said this scam happens every weekend at this
dive; surely you know that."

Her expression didn't change.

I slid out of my seat and looked at her through the still-opened
door. "You should probably investigate your housecleaning staff.
We figure one of them is purposefully unlatching these locks
and their boyfriends are cleaning people out. It's definitely an
inside job."

She blinked, but her expression remained blank. I wondered
if she was in on the scam.

I shrugged and said, "Thanks for the ride. I really love being
taken for a ride." I slammed the passenger door and walked away.

After the pants had been found, we were relieved to find our car keys in a back pocket. Thankfully, the car was in the parking lot, right where he'd left it. We canceled our credit cards, the officers produced a police report and temporary driver's licenses, and we were back on the road by three o'clock that afternoon. The broken drawer was never mentioned.

The adrenaline that had kept me pumped suddenly waned. The drawer-kicker insisted on driving the entire time and my son was attached to his Walkman, so all I had was eight hours of the "what-ifs" and that didn't work out too well. What if I'd awakened and caught them? What if they'd killed us? What if they'd seen me naked? Did they take pictures? What if they'd made copies of our keys — they did have our home address, after all.

I complained to my husband that I couldn't stop thinking about it. He was a mental health therapist, a crisis counselor to be exact, and resourcefully advised me to take my mind back to the Riverwalk in San Antonio where we'd spent a few days during Christmas. Good idea, I thought. So, I created a fantasy, a day-dream, and recalled an architecturally appealing building

I'd noticed and how I'd thought what fun it might be to live on the Riverwalk. Soon, I was another person who not only lived on the top floor of that building, but worked there, too. This new woman started her own business, had a daughter, a grandson and a particularly handsome British lover fashioned somewhat after the looks of Orlando Bloom. The Royal Family was coming to San Antonio and there would be a kidnapping which, of course, my character would solve. It was the most fun I've ever had inside my head!

Talk about happy endings! The next day I related my fantasy to my mother and I mentioned I'd like to find someone to write the book. Her comment? "Why don't you write it?" Me? I thought. It hadn't occurred to me until then that I might actually become a writer. Yet, that's where it all began in 1996. I researched writing, editing, publishing, and joined a writers' group, The Southern Indiana Writers, who have created this book you're reading right now. I wrote that novel, Riverwalk Chameleon, and it sits, resting, until I'm ready to seek publication for it.

Our insurance company replaced everything that had been stolen, and since we'd had a small house fire in February of the previous year, they canceled our homeowner's policy. Evidently people set fire to their own houses, and they fake robberies, so since the insurer can't know for sure who does it on purpose and who doesn't, they just cancel everyone. Oh well. We had to sell the house because we couldn't insure it, but with each new experience, I have done what most fiction writers do, used my life as fodder for stories. I've written a fictionalized story about a burning house, and now I've written my own story about being robbed — burgled, if you want to be precise. I can't even begin to tell you what I did to the motel manager in another story I've written. Perhaps you'll come across it someday and figure it out. I will never again check-in at that particular motel chain, and I'm much more cautious about securing the locks wherever I stay.

I often think of that overused cliché, "When life hands you lemons. . . ." I revised it and came up with this: When life hands you lemons, make Limoncello.

Limoncello—The Perfect Italian Aperitif.

10 organic Meyer lemons
1 liter vodka
3 cups white sugar (if you reduce the sugar by half, the flavor will become more alive)
4 cups water

Zest the lemons, and place zest into a large glass bottle or jar. Pour in vodka. Cover loosely and infuse for seven days at room temperature.

After one week, combine sugar and water in a medium saucepan. Bring to a boil. Boil for 15 minutes. Do not stir. Allow syrup to cool to room temperature.

Stir vodka mixture into syrup. Strain into glass bottles, and seal each bottle with a cork.

Let mixture age for 2 weeks at room temperature.

Place bottled liqueur into the freezer. When icy cold, serve in chilled vodka glasses.

Contributors

The Southern Indiana Writers Group has been more-or-less together since 1992. We began meeting monthly in a conference room in a local hospital. We now meet weekly to exchange information and expertise on everything from computers to poetry. The group also serves as a critique forum (in the same sense that a pack of wolves serves as food critics). Membership is limited, but visitors are welcome, and have been known to fit in so well they become members against their better judgment.

Bonnie Abraham After twenty-five plus years of writing letters disqualifying people from Unemployment Benefits, she retired in order to write something more pleasant. She writes short stories (many with Biblical themes), poetry and devotionals. Currently, she resides in Corydon with her mother's ghost.

Marian Allen lives in a big house in a little wood, which is not the only difference between Allen and Laura Ingels Wilder. She has published stories in print and on-line magazines, including Marion Zimmer Bradley's FANTASY Magazine, The Phone Book, PanGaia and Oceans of the Mind. She blogs at marianallen.com.

Jeannine Baumgartle writes poetry and fiction. Her work has appeared in publications such as *Green Meadow Press*, *Flying Island, Literally*, and Studio: *A Journal for Christians Writing* and won a residency for poetry at the Mary Anderson Center for the Arts . She and her husband live in the small town of Crandall.

Ginny Fleming considers herself to be foremost a screenwriter, as this is her favorite media. Because nobody thought to tell her she couldn't, after optioning 3 scripts for the unsold ensemble sitcom *"Tia"* (any producers reading this?), Fleming dived head-first into the shark-infested mulligan stew (How's that for mixing metaphors?) that is Hollywood scriptwriting. Fleming's take on hysterical fantasy (funny, that is), a novel she likes to call *Dragonsayver* (when she's not calling it Marvin), is a "Shrek-like" novel just begging to be made into an animated film (Fleming wonders if she should shove a tin cup in its hand and drop it on a busy intersection). Besides her annual contribution to SIW anthology and a brief appearance in the Louisville Courier-Journal, Fleming is busy finding a home for *Keys of Illusion*, a Romantic/Suspense novel filled with magic, scuba, fantasy, a bunch of lavender stuff and little bit of sex. Multiple scripts are always in the works whenever Fleming manages to "channel" Jimmy Buffett, her "Muse" (Yeah, she knows Jimmy's not dead — Hopes for his continued good health, in fact — That just makes him easier to channel).

Joanna Foreman was published by Quixote Press in 2008 — a collection of ghost stories—in "Ghosts of Interstate-65."Her stories *Ghost Taxi, Lady of the Wigwam, Vicarious Christmas* have been published by Melange Books in 2011. See www.melange-books.com. Joanna has completed one novel and is currently writing a memoir. While she is not currently a regular blogger, you can visit her website: www.joannaforeman.com and her Facebook Author Page: Joanna Foreman, Author Anti-Blog

Dirk Griffin, also known as The Invisible Man. Dirk is seldom among us in reality, but reality has never been our strong suit, anyway. He has written theatre reviews for Arts Kentuckiana, had a script produced for Public Access Television, and has written music/lyrics and/or scripts for several musicals. Bunbury Theatre of Louisville, Kentucky, selected one of Griffin's plays, *Plastic Jesus*, to include in their 2001 15th Anniversary 15 Minute Play Festival.

T Lee Harris is a writer and illustrator who has been a lover of mystery and the detective genre since discovering books. A graduate of Indiana University with a Bachelor of Fine Arts, T has been involved with radio production, game design, comic books and desktop publishing. Interests include participation in the Society for Creative Anachronism and Renaissance Faires, tailoring authentic costuming for re-enactors and playing online roleplaying games. Several novels are in progress featuring Sitehuti and Nefer-Djenou-Bastet, Josh Katzen and a series set in ninth century Ireland. Work has appeared in print and online venues including mystericale.com and Wildside Press' Cat Tales 2 anthology.

Joy Kirchgessner lives in Corydon with her husband, Mike. Her interests are too vast to list on this page. She's a long-time business woman of Corydon, and artist, whose nature paintings have been accepted into prestigious shows, has achieved the Indiana Lt. Governor's designation of Hoosier Women Artists, photographer, whose photographs have joined her illustrations in our anthologies, equestrian, who enjoys trail rides, amateur archaeologist, who enjoys rock hunting and exploring new worlds — give her a chemistry set and a laboratory and she'd try to split atoms. Many years ago, Southern Indiana Writers tied her to a computer and wonderful stories blossomed from Kirchgessner's many interests. So now, she must add accomplished writer to that long, long list. She even has a novel or two in the early stages.

Glenda Mills resides in New Albany, Indiana with her husband and youngest son. She has a daughter and a son who no longer live at home and one grandchild. When she is not busy homemaking, homeschooling, attending soccer games, running the family taxi service, or volunteering at her church, she writes fiction, nonfiction, and poetry. She looks forward to the day when a person can actually be in two places at once.

Ardis Moonlight quite naturally is a fan of the moon and stars, and finally can see it all in Harrison County, a plus after 32 years in Louisville! A poet with poems published in several issues of "Calliope", an anthology published yearly by Women Who Write, she is also trying her imagination with short stories, and . . . gasp . . . considering a novel!